The Nine
Rules of Credit
What Everyone Needs to Know

Average Joe
SERIES

The Nine
Rules of Credit
What Everyone Needs to Know

Richard Moxley

Self-Counsel Press
(a division of)
International Self-Counsel Press Ltd.
USA   Canada

Self-Counsel Press acknowledges the financial support of the Government of Canada through the Canada Book Fund (CBF) for our publishing activities.

Printed in Canada.

First edition: 2015

Library and Archives Canada Cataloguing in Publication

Moxley, Richard, 1983-, author
    The nine rules of credit : what everyone needs to know / Richard Moxley.

(Average joe series)
Issued in print and electronic formats.
ISBN 978-1-77040-241-6 (pbk.).—ISBN 978-1-77040-996-5 (epub).—ISBN 978-1-77040-997-2 (kindle)

    1. Consumer credit. 2. Finance, Personal. I. Title.

HG3755.M693 2015   332.7'43   C2015-900163-3
                                                        C2015-900164-1

MIX
Paper from
responsible sources
FSC® C004071

Self-Counsel Press
(a division of)
International Self-Counsel Press Ltd.

Bellingham, WA   North Vancouver, BC
USA   Canada

Contents

Chapter Eight
Rule 7: Applying for Credit Lowers Your Score

Chapter Nine
Rule 8: Closing Your Credit Accounts Lowers Your Score

Chapter Ten
Rule 9: Protect Yourself

Chapter Eleven
The Big Picture

Chapter Twelve
Some Important Things to Remember

Conclusion

Tables

Samples

Notice to Readers

Laws are constantly changing. Every effort is made to keep this publication as current as possible. However, the author, the publisher, and the vendor of this book make no representations or warranties regarding the outcome or the use to which the information in this book is put and are not assuming any liability for any claims, losses, or damages arising out of the use of this book. The reader should not rely on the author or the publisher of this book for any professional advice. Please be sure that you have the most recent edition.

Note: The fees quoted in this book are correct at the date of publication. However, fees are subject to change without notice.

Prices, commissions, fees, and other costs mentioned in the text or shown in samples in this book probably do not reflect real costs where you live. Inflation and other factors, including geography, can cause the costs you might encounter to be much higher or even much lower than those we show. The dollar amounts shown are simply intended as representative examples.

Dedication

This book is dedicated to my wife, Jessilyn, who is also my best friend and, of course, to the "monsters" that I love Ben, Ellie, Addisyn, and Joshua. Thank you to the rest of my family for their support and ideas. To everyone else who has influenced my life and the creation of this book; any success I have is because of you.

Introduction

If you live in Canada, it is safe to assume that you are carrying at least one form of debt — credit card, student loan, vehicle loan, and/or mortgage. Even if you don't have any debt, and you live on this continent, you are forced to play the credit game! That's right, a real-life game with rules to follow, strategies for success, penalties for failure, and even personal rankings known as your credit score. How well you play this game will not only determine your interest rates, but also whether you get approved for a property of your own, a place to rent, the premium on your vehicle insurance, a job, or even a parking spot. If you don't know all of the Nine Rules of Credit, no worries — you're the "average Joe" so this book was written for you!

Think you have good credit? You may be paying your bills on time, but what about the other eight rules? If promptness is the only rule you know, what's the likelihood of you wrecking your credit unknowingly? I am not a gambling man, but even I can see that the odds are not good. Is this a chance you're willing to take with so much riding on your credit? You need to learn all the rules in order to play this game well.

For the average Joe, applying for any type of financing can be a scary and complicated process. Let me assure you that I've done everything possible to make this book a completely different experience for you. I think the average Joe learns best through stories so I've tried to demonstrate all my main points with real-life stories based on my clients' experiences (note that the names have been changed to protect my clients' privacy). I have also added some personal stories of my own.

I understand the Rules of Credit and how bankers are trained to think about credit because I've been dealing with them on a daily basis since 2006. I have agents that work at the credit reporting agencies (the companies that rank you on your gameplay) on speed dial, and have met with the underwriters who review loan applications. I have also witnessed thousands of different scenarios that can happen to your credit score, depending on whether you follow the Nine Rules of Credit or not. It doesn't matter if you are just beginning, rebuilding your credit, or trying to maintain the credit you already have. I promise to teach you the inside credit secrets and all the helpful tips I've learned along the way.

"Knowledge is power," as the saying goes. The truth you can learn from this book will not only allow you to always be approved based on your credit, but will also save you hundreds of thousands of dollars over your lifetime. Derek Bok, an American lawyer and educator said it best with this quote, "If you think education is expensive, try ignorance." With the information inside these pages, you will always be able to play the credit game to win.

I also include valuable tips and tools on my websites:

www.TheAverageJoeBook.com

www.eCreditFix.ca

One

Your Credit Report and Score

I was sitting on an overturned bucket in a friend's backyard in a village just outside of Salta, Argentina, when Hermano Gomez asked me if I thought he should apply for a credit card. Are you kidding me? Here? They lived in what would be considered by North American standards to be a shack, with only two rooms with dirt floors, and no indoor plumbing. Gomez had three children and a wife, all crammed into this tiny, tin-roofed home. The taxi my companion and I took to get to this family's house was, I'm sure, one of the first cars ever off the assembly line. The majority of the houses in the area didn't have phones or microwaves, and owning a personal computer was reserved for the very wealthy.

"Why a credit card?" I asked.

"To buy a new television, of course," the family responded.

One thing South Americans share with North Americans is a passion for TV. It is common in South America to see a house without a real door and glassless windows with a satellite dish on the roof so that they can follow their favourite soccer team and watch the occasional Telenovela (Spanish soap opera).

It was 2004 and I had been in rural South America for more than a year. I was becoming accustomed to the carefree lifestyle that the people there enjoyed. Few owned watches; no one had cell phones; there was no such thing as rush-hour traffic; and nobody owed any debt, which made everyone there so much more relaxed. There were no such things as mortgages, loans, or credit cards. That is why I was so shocked when Gomez asked me for advice on credit.

As so many of us do, I repeated to him what my parents told me: "Credit cards are like the devil; fun at first, but they have a tendency to burn you in the end." Maybe I didn't use those exact words, but I had no clue about credit, except that it could be dangerous. It always seemed to be such a huge burden for anyone that became dependent on it. My advice was simply to stay away from credit because like most people, I knew little about it.

When I returned home to Canada in the middle of 2005, I was quickly immersed back into the "real world," where the "buy now, pay later" mentality was the usual way of life. Not long after my return to Canada, I decided to become a mortgage broker. I had advised the wonderful family in Argentina to avoid credit cards and debt all together, and now I was doing a 180-degree turn by helping fellow Canadians get into huge amounts of debt!

I believe that mortgages are a different kind of debt; they are a necessary evil in North America. Most of the top financial gurus call this type of financing "good debt" as opposed to bad debt, which is debt unsecured to a house, a vehicle, or another asset. I personally don't label anything that takes money out of my pocket as a "good" thing, no matter what it may be attached to. The only assets I want to have in my portfolio are ones that continue to put money into my pocket on a regular basis. Of course, my wife and children are the only exceptions to this rule!

Once I started working at a national mortgage brokerage, I learned a lot about finances and even more about credit. Just like most new mortgage agents, it was up to me to find my own clients. I was starting all over again in a brand new industry. Because I am fluent in Spanish, I came up with what I thought was a great idea. I would help Spanish-speaking families with their mortgage financing. I had no problem finding families who wanted to buy their own homes instead of renting them. I was ecstatic about all the success I was having, but then I kept running into one very big problem. Many of my clients had little or no established credit. Even though my niche clients were employed and had managed to save for their down payment, very few banks and mortgage lenders would provide their mortgage financing without them having established credit. It is true that there are programs that allow people to use alternative forms of credit, but these programs are aimed at immigrant families who have been in North America for less than three years.

I continued to work with immigrants but because I needed more business to survive, I also began working with first-time home buyers. I was 23 at the time and I figured that this was the typical age of other young persons who wished to buy their first property. I found many young people interested in purchasing their first home; yet, I ran into the same problem as with my immigrant clients. Although these young people were gainfully employed, and had saved or been gifted money for the down payment, their credit history was limited. Once again, many of the banks and mortgage lenders would not accept people from this category for mortgage financing.

You may think that people from the younger age group or immigrants were the only categories that had problems with credit, and that I would have more success working with those with more life experience. Sadly, I learned that this was not always the case. A person's age seemed to have little bearing on how established his or her credit was. Almost everyone I received an application from was either denied a mortgage because they had no credit history, or they had been forced into higher interest rates due to having bad credit. It became apparent to me that the average person had no clue how to achieve, maintain, or improve his or her credit. It made no difference whether the person was an immigrant, first-time home buyer, or the average Joe.

1. Apply for Your Credit Report

I began to spend more time with my clients reviewing their credit history. I learned that very few had ever seen their own credit report, and no one seemed to know how to improve a poor credit rating.

Credit reports are copies of all your credit account information that is received by both Equifax and TransUnion. Equifax and TransUnion are the two major credit reporting agencies in the world. Their job is to take all the individual credit accounts that you have and then rank you based on a scoring system. Your credit score is also known as a Beacon score, Empirical Credit Scoring, and Fair Isaac Corporation (FICO) score, which are all different names that basically refer to the same thing. They are names which individual companies use to describe how well you are doing at following the Nine Rules of Credit.

Growing up, I was never taught the rules of credit, and any time the subject of credit was brought up, it was usually during a heated debate between my parents that I didn't stick around to hear! Luckily, my father did give me one piece of solid financial advice: "Pay your bills on time." Sound familiar? The problem was that neither my father nor any of the education I received ever taught me about the other eight rules of credit. It's funny how parents can give you such great advice, and then they forget to tell you how to go about achieving it! An even worse case is when your parents or teachers give you outdated or wrong information that they still swear by. I can only imagine what my parents learned about credit in the "good old days"!

After years of reading and reviewing hundreds of credit reports, I realized that TransUnion, Equifax, and even the banks do not think like the rest of us. No wonder going into the bank and applying for credit is such a scary thing for most people to do. The average Joe has no clue why he or she is being denied credit and he or she doesn't know where to begin to find the answers.

Even those who think they have great credit need to know what shows up on their credit report. If you don't know how you got there, or what makes your score go down, you're putting yourself and your financial future at risk.

Until we have a problem with credit, we assume that we know the credit rules already. Most of us are unaware that if we follow some very simple steps, the game of credit would be so much easier to play. How much time would you spend in the penalty box if you were playing hockey, but didn't know the rules? The answer is: too much! While it is true that you can always repair your credit over time — I'm not talking about a five-minute penalty for a major rule violation — it can take six or seven years! Have no fear because when you are armed with insider knowledge, you can either completely avoid the problem or improve your credit at an expedited rate. In the following chapters, I will explain the Nine Rules of Credit in full detail, along with some other important credit and money-saving tips.

If you don't already have a recent copy of both your TransUnion and Equifax credit reports, now would be a great time to apply for them. Here is how you can do that:

For your TransUnion Report (www.transunion.ca), it will cost you $14.95 for your credit report, and $7.95 for your credit score, for a total of $22.90. You can also receive your Consumer Disclosure for free if you apply by regular mail (http://www.transunion.ca/ca/personal/creditreport/consumerdisclosure/mail_en.page).

Visit Equifax to receive a copy of your credit report (www.equifax.ca). You will be given two options. You can order your report with or without the score on it. The report is free if you apply by mail but if you want the total score, it will cost $15.50.

Be very careful when you go on Equifax and TransUnion websites. They make it very difficult for you just to order your credit report and not sign up for a monthly monitoring program. If you want access to your credit report only, or with the score included, you can visit my website (www.TheAverageJoeBook.com) for the direct links to receive copies of your credit reports.

By law, each credit-reporting agency must provide you with one free report, when requested, every 12 months. However, these free copies contain the report only; they don't show your actual credit score. You can go to the credit reporting agencies' respective websites to find an application form, and directions on how to submit your request to each agency. I am frequently asked if it's worth paying the extra money in order to get the score. For the purpose of this book, on learning and understanding where you are in the credit game, I suggest you pay the extra money to know your score. I will go through why your score is important in Chapter 2.

Once you have a copy of both credit reports, go through them in detail to make sure everything is correct and up-to-date. Unfortunately, the credit reporting agencies don't make it easy to read your credit reports; you can visit www.TheAverageJoeBook.com for helpful videos.

2. Credit Score Basics

When you purchase that nice, new 70-inch flat-screen TV with your credit card, all your information is sent electronically to the credit reporting agencies. Every time you make, delay, or miss a payment on any type of account, that information is also recorded. Both TransUnion and Equifax will use that data to determine if you are a credit risk or not. Put in simple terms, you will be ranked depending on how much you will cost a bank or lender. It may be helpful if you imagine your credit score as if it were your Grade Point Average (GPA) from your high school or postsecondary institution. Consider your individual credit accounts, such as credit cards, lines of credit, and loans, as your individual courses.

Your "credit GPA" (credit score), which is the sum of all your accounts, helps potential lenders quickly analyze how you are doing in the credit game. Unlike a GPA, your credit score will be different with each credit-reporting agency, as each company has a different way of grading that same account information. Don't be alarmed by these small variations; just keep in mind that Equifax and TransUnion have slightly different algorithms. (An algorithm is just a fancy word for a computer process that categorizes your information into a format that the average Joe can understand.)

The commonly used saying, "You never get a second chance to make a first impression" is crucial to remember when looking at the importance of your credit score. As banks and lenders review thousands of applications a day, without a high credit score, yours may be put at the bottom of the pile or turned down without someone even going through it. When you hear a student has a 4.0 GPA in school, it gives you the sense that he or she is smart. With your credit score, the higher the score, the better your first impression will be with the bank.

Other than the irregularities in each company's algorithms, your score from either company may be different because not every bank or lender reports to both credit agencies. It costs banks and lenders time and money to submit information to both reporting agencies, meaning some places report to either one or the other. That is why you could have an account show up on one report and not on the other and why it's important for you to request and review both your Equifax and TransUnion credit reports.

For an example of why it is so important to review both credit reports, I will share an experience I had with two of my clients (note that names and small details have been changed to protect my clients' privacy):

Kim and Jerry were referred to me by a financial professional because they were just turned down for a mortgage by their bank due to a low credit score. The couple was devastated that they wouldn't be able to purchase the home that they had been eying even though they were more than qualified in every other aspect. After doing a full in-depth review with them I had some good news.

The bank had only pulled their TransUnion Credit report and the low score was caused by an old Consumer Proposal (a debt relief program similar to Bankruptcy) that wasn't settled properly many years earlier, which shouldn't have showed up after so many years had passed. Jerry's Equifax credit report was 60 points higher than his TransUnion report. It also didn't have any errors on it. The good news is that some banks only focus on the Equifax credit report. I was happy to let Kim and Jerry know that they could get their dream house and I was able to refer them to a mortgage professional who could get the best rate mortgage while we got the TransUnion credit report corrected.

In theory, your credit reports should be mirror images of each other; however, the more time I spend reviewing credit reports the more I realize that having all the information correct is the very rare exception rather than the norm.

On both your Equifax and TransUnion reports, your credit score can range between 300 and 900. I'm sure you have seen many different pictures of ranking scales online, or even on your credit reports. Keep in mind that each type of financing has different guidelines. Mortgage financing is one of the hardest types of credit to qualify for as an average Joe. Therefore, if your credit is considered amazing in the mortgage category, you shouldn't have any issues in any of the others.

A credit score ranking system intended for mortgage financing would look like this:

- Poor 300 – 575

- Fair 576 – 629

- Good 630 – 679

- Excellent 680 – 750

- Amazing 751 – 900

In addition to a bad first impression, your credit score will determine the interest rate or fees that you will be charged. For example, when applying for a vehicle loan, if you have amazing credit or a score (i.e., between 751 – 900), you will get the best, discounted rate. You also won't pay any fees other than the basic set-up fees or other expenses that the seller charges everyone. If you are in the poor or fair credit category, the lenders will apply higher interest rates. The lower your credit score the more it will cost you.

Banks and lenders are a business; they don't lend money to be nice, they do it to maximize profits. A credit score gives them the ability to easily categorize their potential profitability and risk so they can charge you accordingly. To summarize, having a high credit score gives a great first impression and highly influences your cost to borrow.

3. The Importance of Good Credit

Good credit will save you hundreds of thousands, and maybe even millions of dollars, over your lifetime!

I know you may be thinking that the interest rate you qualify for is only 1 or 2 percent higher with bad credit than for good credit, so is the score really that important? You may even be able to afford the higher payments required with a lower score, so what is the big deal?

It is a very big deal. Have you ever been punched in the shoulder — maybe by a friend or an older sibling? The first time it may hurt a bit, but you usually suck it up so you can convince yourself and others that it was no big deal. However, when your older siblings take turns hitting the same spot over and over again those little punches start to add up (obviously I have some unresolved childhood issues)! Think of the banks as your older siblings taking swings at you because your credit is bad. The high interest payments eventually hurt.

The following sections discuss some examples on just how much great credit can save you from getting hurt over your lifetime.

3.1 Mortgages

Vehicle loans, personal loans, lines of credit, and credit cards all work the same way as mortgages. Being charged a higher interest rate may not seem like much on a monthly basis, but over the years it adds up.

Table 1 outlines your savings based on which category of credit you are in. It is based on a $300,000, five-year fixed mortgage, with monthly payments during a 25-year amortization period (e.g., life of the mortgage). The numbers in Table 1 are very conservative for a rate and fee increase with someone who has bad credit.

If you are an average Joe, having more than $150,000 in savings should be incentive enough to always have amazing credit; but hold on, we are just getting started.

With bad credit, not only are you paying higher interest rates, you can also expect to be charged up-front lending fees. Think of these

Table 1
How Your Credit Score Can Influence Your Mortgage Rate

Credit Type	Rate	Monthly Mortgage Payments	Monthly (Savings)	Over 5 Years (Savings)	Over 25 Years (Savings)
Excellent/ Amazing Credit (680 – 900)	3.09%	$1,433.63	$510.83	$30,649.80	$153,249.00
Good Credit (630 – 679)	3.29%	$1,464.75	$479.71	$28,782.60	$143,913.00
Fair Credit (576 – 629)	4.64%	$1,683.85	$260.61	$15,636.60	$78,183.00
Poor Credit (300 – 575)	6.14%	$1,944.46	N/A	N/A	N/A

fees as risk insurance for the lender. The more risky you are, the higher the fee. Depending on how bad your credit is, as well as other qualifying factors, your fees will generally be within 1 to 10 points of the mortgage amount. Whether you keep the mortgage for a year or just a month, you will still pay the same up-front fee.

For example, let's say you had a 550 Beacon score (credit score). Your starting fees would be 3 percent of the entire mortgage amount. On a $300,000 mortgage amount, you are not only paying more than $500 a month, but $9,000 in up-front fees. Isn't that money better in your pocket than in someone else's?

Here's an example to illustrate an average cost of bad credit:

The Robinson family has two mortgages totalling $320,000 on a house that is worth approximately $450,000. They are making monthly payments of $3,250 when they could be paying only $1,529.20 per month, if their credit was good. They are basically throwing away $1,720.80 per month because of not following the Nine Rules of Credit. That means they are paying a total of $103,248 extra over a five-year period, due to higher interest rates. If they didn't improve their credit over that five years, and continued that trend for the life of the mortgage, it would cost them $516,240. This cost is above and beyond the original house price and typical mortgage interest and charges that come along with home ownership.

I am so glad that I graduated from high school knowing how to dissect a frog and how to find the square root of 600, but where was the class on credit? I am not saying that science and math aren't important, but just ask the Robinson's which information would have been more practical.

Money-Saving Tip

Want to have a guaranteed rate of return on your investment? How about making additional payments to your mortgage or vehicle loans? A small lump sum such as $500 a year in extra payments can bring you double-digit savings on interest (note that $500 a year is only $1.37 per day). You can also save money over the long term by switching your loan payments to biweekly or even weekly payments instead of the traditional monthly payments. This forces you to make two to four extra payments a year, which all goes to reducing your debt faster and saves you money.

For prepayment mortgage and loan calculators to estimate how much you can save, go to www.TheAverageJoeBook.com, click Lists & Tools. Under the "Tools" heading you will find "Mortgage Calculators."

3.2 Employment

The list of negatives for having bad credit is endless, but not knowing the Nine Rules of Credit can even prevent you from getting certain jobs or promotions. Accountant certifications and trustees are examples of two professions in which your title can be delayed or taken away based partially on your credit history. Whether it's in a financial institution or any other cash or account handling position, it is common to have a credit check done before you qualify for the job. Employers who perform these credit checks feel that you're less trustworthy if you have bad credit due to incorrect handling of your own finances. Even though there may be extenuating circumstances, any attempt to explain your own poor credit rating may sound like an excuse rather than a legitimate reason.

Beth, one of my clients, is an excellent example of how bad credit limited her earning power. Beth was an accountant and wanted to get a higher certification in the same field but was not able to because of her credit history. Just because she didn't know some of the simple rules of credit, she missed out on her certification and lost an opportunity for a sizable pay increase. In Beth's case, she would have been eligible for a $40,000 per year raise, if only she had better credit. That is a huge amount to lose year after year. During the two years that it will take for her to improve her credit score in order to qualify for the promotion and the higher designation, she will lose $80,000.

3.3 Bad credit restricts options in life

For those who haven't maintained good credit, there is something worse than it costing you more money, and that is less options. In 2008, we saw the banks become much more restrictive on lending practices because of the US subprime meltdown. This financial mess didn't only affect the United States mortgage industry, it put the US into a recession, and almost every other country felt the effects of it. The recession or downturn in the economy put banks and investors on edge, and now everyone has to have better credit than they did before the crisis.

I'm sure if you stop and think about it, you could come up with a few examples of how your options would be limited with bad credit. I'm sure you have thought of setbacks such as not being approved for a mortgage, a vehicle loan, or renting an apartment. These are all true, but here are some additional things that you may not have considered:

- Shopping online by credit card.

- Receiving discounts on your general insurance premiums.

- Setting up a cell phone account.

- Setting up a home security system.

- Hooking up utilities, such as electricity and heat, can be restricted due to a low credit score.

If you don't have a credit card, it makes it hard to do the following:

- Booking a flight.

- Reserving tickets.

- Leasing a vehicle.

- Parking downtown.

Nowadays even your love life can be affected by bad credit. I have clients that have hired me specifically because their bad credit has become an obstacle to continuing in serious relationships. With finances being one of the major causes of relationship break downs, those who have been through previous divorces or separations are asking important financial questions before they get too far in the relationship such as, "How is your credit?"

To be honest, I checked my wife's credit rating before we got married. For me, there is no easier way to see the last six years of someone's financial history beyond his or her credit rating. I'm not saying that those with poor credit don't deserve love as well but it can bring up some great discussions that should be talked about before entering into a serious relationship.

As I've demonstrated, knowing how to achieve and maintain good credit can save you hundreds, thousands, or even millions of dollars. Not having to be restricted or embarrassed in any way, because you've been declined for credit or that promotion you've been working so hard for is priceless!

Now it is time to learn exactly what it takes to have good credit. The following chapters will outline the Nine Rules of Credit that you and every other average Joe should know and review constantly.

Average Joe Action Steps

1. Go to www.TransUnion.ca and request your credit report with your credit score.

2. Go to www.Equifax.ca and request your credit report and your credit score.

3. Review and familiarize yourself with each report. Circle any errors you find. (See Chapter 12 to find out how to correct the errors.)

Two
Rule 1:
Pay Your Bills on Time

Rule 1 is the commonsense rule that I thought I understood until I read my credit report. I then realized I was not as diligent as I should have been. A late payment does hurt your score, and it lowers your score even more with each month it is late.

For example, if you forget to pay your minimum monthly payment, but pay it within a 30-day time frame, it will lower your score, but not near as much if it is not paid within a 60-day time frame. Once you are 90 days late or more, you're really hurting your account and this will continue until you get your account up to date. The more this happens with multiple accounts, or more regularly, the more it will destroy your credit.

1. What If You Have a Good Excuse?

Very rarely do lending companies care about the sequence of events leading up to your delinquent or missed payment. When you signed the contract, you agreed to the conditions.

Nowadays, everything is electronic and computers don't have any sympathy. If you call and speak with an employee, many times he or she has no power to change things already registered in the system. Even if it's a company error, you will still be hard-pressed to get things changed in a timely manner. Loans and lines of credit are the same. It all depends on the policy of each bank, so train yourself to pay early.

2. Tips on How to Remember to Pay on Time

The first step is to know your due date. Note that not all payments are due at the beginning or the end of the month; the due date varies with every card or loan that you have. If, for some reason, the due date is not displayed clearly on the statement, you can call and ask a customer service representative when the payment is due. Don't assume that because you didn't get charged extra interest or some kind of penalty, that it didn't negatively affect your credit. Sometimes a good tearjerker story will convince the service rep to waive the fee or the extra interest, but that doesn't guarantee that it hasn't already been electronically reported on your credit history.

The next step is to devise a way to simplify the process. Money is generally automatically taken out of your account for loans so ensure you have enough money in the account. With credit cards and lines of credit, remembering to pay on time can be a bit harder.

Here is a trick that I use: Pay your regular minimum balance at the very beginning of the month. In order for this to work, you need to know what your minimum monthly payment is, and how it is calculated. Once again, this information can be found on your statement or you can call the customer service agent. For example, if you generally spend $1,000 a month on your credit accounts and your minimum monthly payment is $30, make two payments a month. Make a $30 or $50 payment to cover the minimum payment and then make a payment five business days before your due date to pay the rest of the balance off, if you can. That way, if life gets busy toward the end of the month and you forget, you are guaranteed not to have a late payment show up on your credit report.

You can increase your success rate by automating the payment process. Your bank should have a way to allow you to make automatic payments online or through the branch. If you have all your bills paid automatically, all you have to do is make sure you have enough money in your bank account so you can eliminate late payments. The bills still get paid, even if you are on holidays or you have an emergency. However, under this system, if you change your bank account, you have to ensure that each creditor is made aware of the change.

If you don't want everything automatically paid, you can set a recurring email or an electronic calendar alert to help you keep track of all your different payment obligations. If you are "old school," you can achieve the same results by marking the dates on your paper calendar. However, make sure you do it for the entire year at one time so you don't forget a month.

I frequently get asked if paying down the balance to zero each month will improve a person's credit. As long as the minimum balance is paid each month that is all the lending institutions require. Banks and credit card companies don't want you to pay back what you owe all at once because the longer it takes, and the higher your balance is, the more money they make. Obviously, my suggestion would be to pay your balance in full each month to avoid paying high interest rates.

One strategy to help build your credit faster is to make multiple payments on your card each month. This won't increase your credit score, but it builds a positive relationship with your lender. Bank reps have also confirmed to me that the more payments you make each month, the more favourable it looks on the banks' internal processes, especially with loan payments.

Money-Saving Tip

Most credit card companies will charge 18 to 28 percent interest 21 days from the time you make a purchase. The time between when you make a purchase and when the interest is applied is called your grace period. Making a payment at the end of the month even if you pay the full balance will still cost you high interest on the balances that you have carried on your credit card for more than 21 days. To insure you understand the terms and conditions, find the original contract that you received when you signed up or you can call the number on the back of your card to find out exactly what your grace period is from the customer service centre.

3. The Bills That Show up on Your Credit Report

It is also important to know what is on your credit report. Suppose you find yourself in a financial bind and you have to choose which bills you're going to pay first that month. You should pay the bills that will affect your credit the most. By no means am I suggesting that you shouldn't pay certain bills, but if there are times when extreme circumstances arise, such as an illness, death in the family, or loss of employment, you may have to make choices. During these times, when you can't pay all your bills, it's good to know that bills such as rent, heat, hydro, water, phone, cable, and taxes don't affect your credit score right away. However, if these bills go unpaid for a number of consecutive months, they will be sent to collections.

Collection companies specialize in finding and collecting outstanding debts and provide services on behalf of the banks and lenders. Once your bill is with a collection company, it will immediately register the black mark on your credit report. The collection shows up under the public records portion of your credit report where you will also see any bankruptcies, consumer proposals, and all the rest of the biggest negative hits to your credit. Public records including collections really hurt your credit. Unfortunately, paying the collection doesn't remove the damage it has done because a collection will stay on your credit report six years from the time it was first registered.

You may be surprised how many people have collections recorded on their credit reports. Most times people don't even realize it. They usually find out when they apply for some type of financing.

The hardest part about discovering that you have a collection reported when you're applying for financing is that it can ruin your chances of approval, or at least cost you higher interest or fees. Either way, it is something most lenders will want confirmation it is paid before they will provide you with additional financing. The easiest way to confirm payment is by receiving a letter confirming that the account has been settled in full or the account balance is now at zero. Please make sure you keep this letter for at least six years as collections have been known to come back on your report even after you have paid.

If you have paid the collection and it is still showing up with a balance, please visit www.TheAverageJoeBook.com for services available to have it removed quickly.

4. What Happens When You Don't Make Your Mortgage Payments?

Your mortgage payment doesn't always show up on your credit report, but if you are late on multiple payments, it could affect the interest rate you're offered from the bank when your mortgage comes up for renewal again. If you miss three consecutive payments or more in a row, it will lead to foreclosure proceedings, which is when the bank or lender starts the process of legally taking ownership of your property due to the lack of payments. Banks or lenders don't want to own your home, but if the lender isn't getting paid, it will try and sell the property in order to reduce its losses. Foreclosure shows up under the public record portion of your credit report.

You may assume that bankruptcy is the worst thing you can do for your credit; however, if you are applying for mortgage financing, going through a foreclosure is the absolute worst thing you can do for your credit. Bad credit can be rebuilt fairly quickly, but very few lenders will look at providing financing for you if you have a previous foreclosure showing up on your credit report, regardless how strong your current credit is.

If you find yourself in a situation where you may not be able to make your mortgage payments, contact your mortgage lender or mortgage agent to find out what can be done. The same thing is true with any creditor. If you don't think you'll be able to make a payment to any one of your creditors, it is a good rule of thumb to contact them to see if something can be worked out, especially if you contact them before the due date. I've never seen the attitude of pretending it will all go away actually work for anyone.

I understand that despite your best efforts, an emergency may come up, preventing you from being able to make a payment. However, the banks still feel that it is your responsibility to keep track of your accounts and pay your bills on time. Get your head around this rule and you will have a great foundation to always have amazing credit.

Money-Saving Tip

If you find it difficult to cover all your expenses in a month, there are two ways to correct this:

- Option 1: Reduce your expenses. You may already believe you are sacrificing more than anyone else but you can reduce your expenses. The key is to review your monthly statements and know exactly where all your money is going. Monitor regularly to see what is essential and what can be reduced.

- Option 2: Increase your income. You can work overtime or find out how you can get a pay increase in your current job. The one idea I have seen be most successful is starting a part-time business. It might reduce your TV time but a part-time business can be fun, and bring in extra money with little or no increase in paying taxes. You can turn your hobby into a money-making passion. If you don't have a business idea, you can always look for a pre-existing business to partner with or join.

Average Joe Action Steps

1. Come up with a system that works for you to either automate your bill payments, or know when each bill payment is due.

2. Consider which bills you could possibly make multiple payments toward each month.

3. Review your bank and credit card statements to see where all that money is going.

Three

Rule 2:
High Balances Equal
Low Scores

When people hear that they should stay away from high balances, they tend to think about the total amount of money they owe. However, the credit-reporting agencies, TransUnion and Equifax, are more concerned about how much you owe in contrast to what your limit is, also known as loan-to-value (LTV).

Credit-reporting agencies use your LTV, shown as a percentage, as an indicator of how well you manage your credit. For example, if you have a limit of $500 on your credit card or line of credit, and your balance owing is $400, your balance is deemed too high. This same $400 balance, with a card limit of $2,000, is considered a low balance.

1. What Gives You a High Balance?

What actually constitutes a high balance on your credit accounts? I've seen different sources state anything more than 20 percent and up to 75 percent utilization of your limit is deemed as high credit balance.

Official statements from Equifax and TransUnion differ in what they consider a high balance.

TransUnion's website states very clearly that any balance higher than 50 percent of the limit will harm your credit, and it even suggests aiming for as low as 30 percent loan-to-value. For example, if your line of credit has a limit of $1,000, every time the bank reports the information to TransUnion, your balance had better be less than $500, or it will lower your credit score.

Equifax's current website doesn't mention any specific ratios. However, its old website says, "Try not to run your balances up to your credit limit. Keeping your account balances below 75% of your available limit will help your score."

If you want to get technical, any balance of more than 8 percent of your limit will cause you to start losing a few points. However, after reviewing thousands of Equifax and TransUnion credit reports I have found that any balance less than 50 percent wasn't hurting the score very much. It was only when the balance is between 50 and 75 percent of its limit that it started lowering the consumers' credit score where it would affect their ability to qualify for financing. Scores really start taking a hit when the loan-to-value ratio or the balance is higher than 75 percent of the limit. Obviously, the lower the percentage the balances are compared to the limit the better; however, I always advise my clients to never use more than half of their limits.

One thing everyone seems to agree on is that maxed-out balances or having a balance close to the max will drop your score a lot. It makes practical sense not to have balances close to the limit as it will only increase the chances of mistakes being made. If you ever miss a payment, or if you go over your limit, it will drop your score immensely. It doesn't matter if it was a $500 limit or a $50,000 limit, living on or around the limit makes you appear risky to banks.

Whenever I talk about this rule in one of my live presentations, someone always claims that for him or her it is OK to max out his or her credit during the month because he or she pays off the balance in full before the due date. Although it is great to pay off your account in full each month, lenders send your account information electronically once every 30 to 90 days to the credit reporting agencies. When your individual account information is sent to Equifax and TransUnion differs with each institution and won't necessarily line up with your due date. Even if you are diligently paying your balances off in full each month, your credit will still take a hit. The trick is to keep your balances low all the time. If you have trouble keeping your balances at less than 50 percent of the credit limit on all your credit accounts, then either increase your limits, or move part of the balance to another credit card or line of credit.

Money-Saving Tip

It is advantageous to have credit established with different banks. This in no way will help increase your credit score; however, it can save you financially to have a history with more than just one bank. For example, I personally have accounts with two of the major banks. The credit card that I have with each of these companies offers special rates for switching balances from one to the other. This trick helps me save money with more than just credit card financing. Banks are more willing to give you their best discounted rates if they can steal some sort of business from a different bank. Competition between lenders assures you that you will get the lowest rates available.

My clients, John and Cathy, who were planning to buy their first home, are good examples of the importance of Rule 2 — high balances equal low scores. Although, they had tried to save enough money for a down payment, they didn't have enough for the typical 5 percent down. At that time, in 2006, banks had access to a program that offered 100 percent financing. The kicker was that they had to have a credit score of at least 680.

A few months prior to their application for a mortgage, both John and Cathy had credit scores a little more than the 680 mark, but by the time I pulled their credit report again, it had dropped more than 50 points for Cathy and 40 points for John. Even though they had a great repayment history, their last purchase had put them $25 over their $500 limit. As John and Cathy had already picked out the house they wanted and given notice to their landlord, they were now in trouble. The couple looked at getting a cosigner (another applicant brought on to the mortgage to strengthen it) to help, but any willing family members were either not living in the country or not in a position to help. When I spoke to the lender, I was told it couldn't make an exception due to the over-the-limit balance of $25. The two could have easily paid the debt owing on the card, but because the over-the-limit amount showed up on their credit report, the bank felt they were not in control of their finances and refused to lend them the money. This left John and Cathy no other choice than to continue renting until they could get their credit scores back up to the 680 mark.

I work with many clients trying to rebuild their credit score and I've noticed that the lower the limit on your credit card, the harder it is for the average Joe to stay under the 50 percent mark. With a limit of $500 or less it doesn't take long to start hurting your credit by having a high balance. You can avoid this issue regardless of your limit. Get in the habit of only using the credit card for small items and then use cash, debit, or a different credit card for the other purchases.

2. Loans and High Balances

I've been talking mostly about credit cards and lines of credit, but there is another popular form of credit and that is a loan. Loan balances are much harder to keep at 50 percent or less of your limit. Think about it: If you apply for a loan, your limit is your balance at day one, and this will lower your score. It is irrelevant to your credit what you paid for a vehicle or how much cash you used for a down payment on your entertainment system. With loans, the lender will only report what your original loan amount was and what your current balance is. It is only until you reach the halfway point of your term that your credit score stops being lowered due to the high balance.

Although having a loan balance of more than 50 percent of your limit doesn't lower your score as much as it does with a credit card or a line of credit, it still has a negative effect. If you have the means to qualify for the full amount, and then prepay the balance down to the halfway mark, this would be a great way to build your credit. Unfortunately, the majority of people applying for a loan don't have the resources to prepay a loan more than the minimum set payments.

Some readers may be upset because no one ever warned them about this before. Who would have guessed that Equifax and TransUnion would rank being approved for a new loan as a negative hit to your credit score?

To be honest, there are pros and cons with each type of credit, and I go through these in more detail throughout the book. However, Rule 2 still stands, and you have to realize that with any type of credit, any balance over the halfway mark will lower your credit score.

Average Joe Action Steps

1. Review your history with your credit accounts and see if you used more than 50 percent of your credit limits in any of your credit accounts.

2. If you do sometimes go over the 50 percent mark, call your lender and ask if it will increase your limit so you won't go over 50 percent anymore.

3. If your bank won't increase the limit, see about spreading some of your debt to other accounts.

Four

Rule 3:
You Must Have
Established Credit

As important as having a high credit score is, even with an amazing credit score, you can still be declined access to additional credit of any kind. You may be scratching your head wondering why you wouldn't be approved, even though your credit score is soaring. There are two other aspects, along with the credit score that banks look at before they will consider you to have good credit. The first is how long you have had each account established; the second is how high the limits are for each one.

1. It Takes Time to Build Your Credit

Think of it this way: To obtain any kind of financing the lender looks for assurance that you are going to pay back the money. If you have few mistakes on your credit history, the bank will proceed with a bit of caution. However, with no current history, the bank will find you more risky due to the fear of the unknown. If the bank has nothing to rank you on, you won't be offered the best discounted rates, you will be requested to pay a higher down payment, charged extra fees, or be declined.

Have you ever loaned someone a large sum of money? Would you give someone you barely know $500, $4,500, or even $10,000? I loaned a family member a large sum of money once. I based my decision on the fact that I knew she could be trusted. The bank doesn't actually know you unless you have a prior established relationship. Even if you've dealt with the bank before for savings or investments, it will still want to see a repayment history when it comes to debt.

The keyword for lenders is "history." With this family member that I dealt with, I was the bank and I had already established a history with her. I lent her the money because I knew her spending habits; I had witnessed her work ethic while growing up; and I knew she was honest and would keep her word. If she said she was going to pay me back, I knew she would.

If I don't know someone and/or can't see his or her repayment history, there is no way I'd lend my money to that person. The bank feels the same way. Unless you are being charged more for rates or fees, no one wants to be the first person to lend you money when you don't have a repayment history.

2. Secured Credit

You may be thinking that if no one wants to be the first. Then how is it possible to start building or rebuilding a history? That is an excellent question. The best answer would be to apply for a secured credit card. You can secure the credit card to your house, to investments, or to plain cash. With a secured credit card $500 is the usual starting limit. This amount can be increased based on other assets and strengths on your application. Secured credit cards are great tools for building or rebuilding your credit. Think of this card exactly like a credit card, but with a required security deposit (similar to when you rent). It is attached to your personal name, you get monthly statements, there's a minimum payment, and the company is even nice enough to charge you interest! Your deposit is held as security until you close your account or until the company decides you are no longer a risk and refunds your deposit back to you.

Unfortunately, in the last couple of years, major banks have made it more apparent that they don't want to issue many secured credit cards. They will still offer them to those people who are young and just starting out, or to those who are immigrants. However, those seeking to rebuild their credit will have to be approved by a non-banking institution.

Non-bank lenders, who specialize in dealing with those with bruised credit history, will be around the same interest rates as an unsecured credit card (19 to 24 percent). The reason the fees and interest rate are similar is because the up-front cash or security minimizes the bank's risk. If you don't make your payments, eventually it will take your security deposit. Remember, if you are late or don't make your payments, your credit will be affected in the same negative way as outlined in Rule 1 — pay your bills on time.

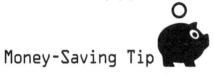

Money-Saving Tip

Some credit companies will allow you to secure a portion of the limit rather than the whole amount. This way you won't have to cough up as much money up front. For example, it is better to only have to put $300 down as a security on a $500 limit as this will leave you free to spend the other $200 as you wish. With this scenario, you can then get two credit cards by tying up only $600. I go through the importance of having at least two credit accounts active further on in section 5. Although it may seem weird to have $600 secured in order to have access to $1,000 of credit, this is where you have to start to establish your credit. As you build a credit history with a company, it will increase your limit over time without any more money being required for security.

3. Prepaid versus Secured

Please note that there is a difference between a secured credit card and a prepaid one. A prepaid credit card does not improve or harm your credit in any way. It is like a gift card that is paid for in advance and can be used until the total amount is spent. There are no monthly payments, and it doesn't have anyone's name attached to it.

Some people just starting out, who are 18 or older, have no problem being approved for a credit card. They probably don't have a credit score, but they have had some type of history with a bank. Due to this fact, they will generally be approved for a student card or some type of basic credit card without too much hassle. Everyone else, including those who are immigrants, will either have to prove an established credit history or have assets to offset the increased risk for the bank.

The good news is that if you get turned down by a major bank, there are usually lots of other options. Just turn on the radio or television and there will always be a lender advertising that your approval will be guaranteed. Most of the time, you don't even have to go looking for one. You will either receive an application in the mail, or be harassed to apply for one at the bank, the mall, the grocery store, or just about anywhere else you can think of!

When re-establishing your credit, vehicle loans will be the easiest form of credit to qualify for. Once again, because the loan is attached to an asset, there is a reduced risk to the lender, so it is more likely that you will be approved.

4. How Long Does It Take to Establish or Re-establish Your Credit?

According to the credit agencies, it takes four to five years for each account to be deemed established. TransUnion's website states: "The age of the oldest account on your file is a good indicator of how much credit experience you have. If your oldest account is more than four to five years old, you are considered to have solid credit experience. If your oldest credit account is less than that, other factors such as the number of accounts and type of accounts will be more important in determining your ability to manage credit." Equifax, as well, confirms that the longer you have an account, the more established your credit appears.

Each bank and lender will have its general approval guidelines, separate from what the credit reporting agencies would consider ideal. Generally, if you have no credit, you will need to establish it for one year before you qualify for most types of financing. If you had poor credit previously, they would prefer to see two years of re-established credit before the major banks will offer you the best rate for financing.

Keep in mind that although there will always be someone who will approve you, the better established your credit the better the interest rate you will receive and the less it will cost you in fees and monthly expenses.

Some readers may be surprised by how short a time it takes for them to re-establish their credit. Many have the misconception that just because they have bruised credit, they are unable to get approved for any type of credit until it is removed from their report. That is not the case. See Table 2.

Table 2
Lenth of Time Negative Information Will Stay on Your Credit Reports

Type of Information	Equifax (Years)	TransUnion(Years)
Late payments	6	6
Collections (from date of missed payment)	6	6
Bankruptcy (from date of discharge for BC, AB, SK, MB, NS, NT, YT, NU)	6	6
Bankruptcy (from date of discharge for ON, QC, NB, PE, NL)	6	7
Consumer proposal or orderly payments of departments (from date of discharge)	3	3
Legal judgments (e.g., lawsuits) for BC, AB, SK, MB, NS, NT, YT, NU	6	6
Legal judgments (e.g., lawsuits) for ON, QC, NB, NL	N/A	7
Legal judgments (e.g., lawsuits) for PE	10	7

Yes, it is true that credit counselling or even bankruptcy will stay on either credit report between two and seven years. However, please keep in mind that the bank and your credit score are almost entirely weighed on the last couple of years, regardless of any previous problems. Also, please note that the clock starts ticking from the time you are discharged (paid your bankruptcy or credit program in full).

The point is that if you are building or rebuilding your credit, it is time to start now. That way, it should take you between one and two years to have your credit re-established enough to qualify for the best rates once again.

Nick and Melissa are great examples of how two years of re-established credit is the key. Once these clients entered bankruptcy, they began actively seeking education on how to qualify for a mortgage again. Because they received the right information about re-establishing their credit, very early in the process (as soon as they had completed paying for their bankruptcy), they qualified for a 5 percent down payment and the best rate, within two years.

If you are considering going bankrupt a second time, please do everything you can to not let that happen. Banks and lenders are less forgiving of people who have previously gone bankrupt. Also Equifax states, "If the consumer declares several bankruptcies, the system will keep each bankruptcy for fourteen (14) years from the date of each discharge." A double bankruptcy is the kiss of death to the banks and you will be very hard-pressed to get best-rate financing during the 14 years. If you are in this situation, talk to your bankruptcy trustee about a consumer proposal instead of going into a second bankruptcy, which can stop you from having this negative hit on your credit report for so long.

Please note that no matter what type of financing you apply for, depending on your specific financial situation, you may be able to acquire financing before the usual waiting period is over.

5. Credit Limits and Mortgage Financing

Mortgage financing is one of the hardest types of financing to get approval. Unlike business financing, the majority of people will go through mortgage financing multiple times during their life.

Banks now want to see that you can handle higher limits on your credit before approving you for a mortgage. This makes sense as the amount the average North American is borrowing, especially for mortgages, continues to increase.

Let's say you have always managed a $500 credit limit on your credit card. This is a great start. However, there is a huge difference between missing the $15 minimum monthly payment and a $1,000 or $2,000 monthly payment on a mortgage. That is why, along with a great credit score, the banks are looking for evidence that you can control large amounts of credit.

The banks aren't just referring to having one established account either; they want to see at least two to three. Each of these credit accounts (i.e., credit card, line of credit, or loan from any bank or lender) should have limits of at least $2,500.

Here is how I first learned about the importance of having higher credit limits. In June 2009, I ran into a situation with my client, Alex, who had one active credit card with a limit of $1,500, and the lender said that it wasn't high enough. I was shocked when I heard that the lender wanted his limit to be at least $2,500. That condition didn't come from a specific bank either. It came from the Canadian Mortgage and Housing Corporation (CMHC), a Crown corporation that came into existence mainly to make mortgage money more accessible to the average person.

Genworth Canada and Canada Guarantee are both private corporations and competitors with CMHC, but they only own a very small percentage of the market share. Currently, any person who wishes to put less than a 20 percent down payment on a mortgage needs the approval of any one of these three main insurers. There are banks and lenders that self-insure; they don't go through one of the three major insurers. However, these self-insured lenders are non-major lenders known as private or B-lenders. These lenders fill the need for those who don't meet the higher requirements of mainstream banks.

The current guideline being used by the three main insurers is to have at least a credit limit of $2,500 on two credit accounts in order for someone to have established credit. Because Alex's credit didn't meet CMHC's guidelines, he required an additional $24,000 for a down payment. Luckily, his father was able to give him the extra money, and shortly after that, he increased his limits on his credit cards.

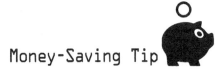

Money-Saving Tip

When looking for mortgage financing ask a mortgage professional for ways that you can save money with an insurer. For example, having a 10 percent down payment instead of 8 percent can save you a couple thousand dollars. Other savings can be realized when you reduce your amortization (i.e., life of the mortgage).

6. Types of Accounts That Don't Build Your Credit

Cell phone accounts never used to be shown on your credit report but now they show up on both your Equifax and TransUnion credit reports. On the TransUnion report, your cell phone account does show up, and it is used to calculate your credit score. With Equifax, the account is tracked but it does not help your credit score. Regardless how it is reported, banks and lenders do not consider cell phone accounts as a serious bill payment. Although it doesn't hurt to have it on your credit, don't use it as a way to start, rebuild, or maintain great credit.

This also goes for student loans. It will only help you establish a credit score on your TransUnion credit report but not on your Equifax. No banks or lenders consider student loans as established credit.

Bank account information doesn't show up on your credit as it isn't credit. This includes debit MasterCards and debit Visas. Overdraft accounts attached to those accounts are a form of credit. These accounts can show up on a credit report, but once again they don't help establish your credit.

As well intended as any advice may be, you have to be careful what information you trust. I have parents tell me all the time that they would like their son or daughter to qualify for a mortgage in order to build his or her credit. Not that this is a bad thing, but mortgages don't build your credit score. Equifax confirms this on its reports. Equifax says, "Mortgage information may appear in your credit report, but is not used to calculate your credit score."

If you have a home equity line of credit (i.e., line of credit attached to your house), or if a line of credit is combined with a mortgage, most likely it will show up on your credit report because the majority of lending institutions will report it. The home equity line of credit will report and established your credit and contribute to your credit score like a regular line of credit. All mortgages with good repayment histories will help you build a relationship with the current institution that holds that mortgage. However, it won't help your credit score.

The previous couple of examples won't always help build your credit, but they can hurt it. For example, if you don't pay your cell phone bill or make your mortgage payment as scheduled, the lender will eventually send the cell phone bill to a collections company, or put your mortgage into foreclosure, which will hurt your credit.

Average Joe Action Steps

1. If you haven't started building or rebuilding your credit, get a plan in place and start now.

2. If you don't already have at least two credit accounts with limits of $2,500 each, apply for them.

3. If you are using mortgages, cell phones, overdrafts, or student loans to build your credit, repeat the second step above.

Five

Rule 4:
Some Types of Credit Are Better Than Others

Many of my clients ask me which bank or type of credit is better. My answer is that it depends on you. There are three important considerations before deciding which works best for you:

1. Be honest with yourself. Look at the pros and cons and see which option will help you achieve active and established credit, but also won't put you further into debt. For example, if a credit card with a limit of $2,500 or higher will get you into trouble, then it's not worth having. If you're just maintaining a loan in order to keep your credit active, try an investment loan so at least you will be increasing your financial position while you're improving your credit. Talk to your financial planner for further details on investment loans and if they are right for you.

2. Compare the selling features of each option because some may have a higher interest rate, but allow you more flexibility.

3. Read the fine print. Just because you get an introductory rate or reward points, it may not be worth the yearly fees. Unfortunately, as consumers, we get so caught up in one feature that we don't take the time to understand what the costs associated with it are. As the old adage states: "To be forewarned is to be forearmed."

My objective in this chapter isn't to tell you which bank or lender is better, rather, it is to explain the different types of credit available to you as well as their pros and cons. The three most important types of credit accounts are: Revolving, Installments, and Open.

You may have heard from some "credit gurus" that it is really important to have all types of credit, such as loans, revolving credit, and open credit, in order to establish good credit. Both of the reporting agencies, Equifax and TransUnion, allude to this commonly misunderstood statement on their websites. TransUnion's website says that, "A healthy credit profile has a balanced mix of credit accounts and loans." Equifax also makes a brief reference to this on some of its personal credit reports. Equifax states that, "Generally the more diversified in industry and types of accounts you have, the higher your score is."

When I sit down with my clients to provide them with a customized plan for them to rebuild or improve their credit the fastest way possible, it always includes using revolving credit (i.e., credit cards and lines of credit) and will almost never include using loans unless under special circumstances.

Why don't I follow the "others" including Equifax and TransUnion's advice? When you are taking advice from anyone you have to understand the whole picture in order to understand the context. For example, I always remember my dad saying, "It doesn't matter how much money comes into your business, or what is on your paycheque, it only matters how much stays in your pocket." He ran a paving company and he had government and private contracts that ran into the millions. When the average Joe hears big numbers like "millions" or "hundreds of thousands" of dollars, he or she would assume that things are going really well. However, if you look at the whole picture, even if you are bringing in a billion dollars, you aren't getting ahead if you have a billion in expenses.

The algorithm (computer code) that determines your credit score adds positive points for having multiple forms of credit (e.g., credit cards, lines of credit, loans, and open accounts such as a cell phone).

However, this makes up less than 5 percent of your credit score. If you have great credit, it is a waste of time applying for other forms of credit that have extra fees or interest costs that will only raise your credit score a few points. When rebuilding your credit, banks and lenders want to see revolving credit accounts (e.g., credit cards and lines of credit) as they are the most tempting for the average Joe and the hardest to maintain. If you handle revolving credit properly, you should be able to be responsible with all the other forms of credit as well.

To be clear, I'm not suggesting that you should never apply for a loan or a cell phone account, but these forms of credit should not be the priority form of credit used to rebuild or maintain great credit. The most important part of this chapter is to explain the pros and cons of all types and for you to use the method of credit that works best for you. Follow the Nine Rules of Credit, regardless of what type of credit you use and you will be good to go!

1. Revolving Credit Accounts

Revolving credit accounts include credit cards and lines of credit (unsecured or secured to assets such as property, investments, or cash). The payment fluctuates depending on the interest rate, balance owing, and type of account you have.

1.1 The pros of revolving credit

I like revolving accounts because you can pay down and reuse them whenever you want. This is very helpful if you need money for a short-term period. You can use what you need and then pay it down again as soon as you get paid or the money becomes available. The payments are generally lower than that of an installment (loan) type account because it is common for them to have interest-only or low-payment requirements. If you have interest-only payments, you will never pay off the debt unless you make additional contributions to the account. Even revolving accounts that include a balance pay-down portion in your payments will still take years to pay your debt. For example, on a credit card balance of $5,000, you are looking at around 40 years to pay it down to $0 when making your minimum payments only.

The following are the pros of revolving credit:

- **Credit cards:** My favourite part about credit cards is that the only time you pay interest on them is when you don't pay your balance off before the grace period (generally 21 days from a purchase). This allows you the convenience of using the card and always keeping your credit active, without being forced to pay any interest at all. If you travel a lot, they are great to have, and of course, there are reward points on most cards.

- **Lines of credit:** If you carry debt from month to month, I suggest that a line of credit would be better for you. The interest rate that you will be charged will be much less than that of credit cards. Although a line of credit is not as flexible as a credit card, you can still transfer money from account to account instantly.

- **Secured line of credit:** This type of credit is exactly the same as a line of credit, but because it is attached or secured to some kind of asset (e.g., house or investment), your interest rate is usually a bit lower. There are also some banks who will give you a debit card with this account, which helps you have easy access to your credit. Depending on the worth of the asset, you can also have larger limits. This is because, if you don't make your payments, the lender can take your asset to cover the balance of the debt.

1.2 The cons of revolving credit

Temptation! Although ease of access is one of the pros to revolving credit, for the average Joe without strong will power, it could become a problem. The combination of ease of access and low-minimum payments is just too much for some people. Just read the financial section of any newspaper and you will find that many North Americans are going further into debt. Revolving credit is not the problem; the problem is that there is a lack of education when it comes to money and being responsible with credit.

The following are the cons of revolving credit:

- **Credit cards:** A lot of times, in exchange for more points, or to be offered a lower interest rate, credit card companies may charge you an annual fee. I don't suggest that you go this route because you can get reward cards without paying fees, and if you are carrying balances, you should use a line of credit instead.

- **Line of credit:** Daily compounding interest means that from the moment you have a balance you will be charged interest on a daily basis. In other words, for a very short-term debt, it will be less expensive to utilize your credit cards. For example, you have planned a vacation to a tropical destination and you have to pay for it now to reserve the booking. If you don't have all the money right now but you will shortly, it would be better to pay for it with a credit card than with your line of credit. With the credit card, you have 21 days (depends on the card) from the time you make a purchase before the interest is charged. With the line of credit, even though the interest rate isn't as high as the credit card, the interest charged is based on the balance of each day.

- **Secured lines of credit**: Many people find themselves in trouble because, unlike a credit card or line of credit that generally has a limit of $10,000 or less, it is not uncommon to see secured credit with limits of $100,000 plus. That is more than most people make in a year. Just to clarify, it isn't the higher limit amount that is bad; rather, it is that there is more temptation to utilize higher debt amounts. The more debt you have, the higher your minimum monthly payment will be and the harder it is to pay it off.

2. Installment Accounts

Every type of loan falls under the category of installment accounts. Your payment is based on a set term that has part interest and part principle pay down. Unlike revolving credit, you can't withdraw any more money on the loan unless you go through the application and approval process first.

2.1 The pros of installment accounts

When using this type of account, it takes a conscious decision to get into more debt, in addition to being approved by a lender to increase your balance. Loan payments will have a term associated with them. A term is the maximum length of time it will take you to pay off the loan (except with mortgages), based on the interest rate, payment schedule, and the terms and conditions found in your contract. This means there is a light at the end of the tunnel; any extra payments you make above and beyond your minimum required amount will simply shorten the length of the loan.

The following are the pros of using installment accounts:

- **Personal loan:** The nice thing about a personal loan is that you don't have to secure it to anything. It can be used to consolidate debt or to buy something that is not an asset.

- **Secured loan:** Vehicle and investment loans, along with mortgages, fall under the secured loan category. Generally, the interest rate will be better, and it is easier to qualify for because of reduced risk to the lending institution. Remember, mortgages, even if they show up on your credit report, do not build your credit. No one has ever been able to give me a good reason why a mortgage loan doesn't build your credit score, but currently it doesn't.

2.2 The cons of installment accounts

The biggest reason why I personally don't like to use loans when accessing credit is because 99 percent of the time, you are forced to pay some type of interest. There are generally application or administration fees involved to open or close an installment account. As discussed in Rule 2, loans are harder to keep the balance at 50 percent or less of your limit. Generally, once you have been approved for a loan, your balance is your limit, and your score will be lowered because of it. With each payment you make, it will lessen the impact on your credit until you are about halfway through your term. At this point, the loan will start to improve your credit again.

The following are the cons of installment accounts:

- **Personal loans:** They are harder to qualify for and they come with a higher interest rate than secured loans.

- **Secured loan:** Although the loan interest rates are lower than credit cards, sometimes, there are restrictions to making extra payments. Keep in mind, paying a slightly higher interest rate can be worth having the flexibility of an early repayment option.

3. Open Accounts

There has been some confusion about open accounts in the past as some sources consider lines of credit and student loans to fall under this category. However, an open account is simply a credit card or an account; you can borrow money as needed and the total balance is due at the end of each period, generally monthly. For those readers who were around before credit cards became popular, it may be helpful to think of an open account as a charge card or Diners Club card. For those of you scratching your head because you have never heard of such cards, let me use a different example. Cell phone accounts today are the most common type of open account.

3.1 The pros of open accounts

Open credit is very different from the revolving type, but it shares the benefit of convenience. It looks and acts the same as any credit card that allows you the flexibility to buy/use what you want when you want it. The other main benefit is that you don't have a limit. Think of this type of credit as the Autobahn (Freeway) in Germany, which advises a "recommended speed" of 130 kilometres per hour but there is no actual speed limit.

The following are the pros of open accounts:

- **Charge cards:** Using a charge card instead of a revolving credit card would allow you to discard Rule 2! The reason you could disregard Rule 2 on any open type account is because it is impossible to utilize more than 50 percent of your limit, when there is no limit. This would be a good option for those of you who put large amounts on your credit card, but faithfully pay it off at the end of each month.

    Cell phone accounts: There are a couple of benefits to having a cell phone contract, as opposed to a prepaid contract. First, there are only a few types of prepaid cell phones so your selection is limited. Second, the benefit is that you don't have to go to a corner store to buy more minutes. This way you will never miss an important phone call.

3.2 The con of an open account

There is one very important con to consider when it comes to open accounts:

- Charge cards: If you think an interest rate between 18 to 24 percent is bad, try the typical 30 percent if you don't pay your charge card balance off in full each month. Not only are you charged a high interest rate, but there is no such thing as a minimum payment. This means that if the balance isn't paid off 100 percent each month, it will be registered as a late payment. That is why open accounts are very rare and most credit card companies and banks don't even offer them.

4. Home Equity Lines of Credit (HELOC) versus Mortgage

I am constantly asked if home equity lines of credit (HELOC) are a good choice; my answer again would be that it all depends. If you are unfamiliar with HELOC, think of it as a line of credit that is attached to your mortgage. You can use it up to the limit and pay it off as you please without any additional financing. You can have it instead of a mortgage or in combination with one.

You need to review the pros and cons of each type of credit and decide which will help you best achieve your financial goals. I would also suggest you talk with a mortgage professional as part of the process of educating yourself on both options. This may help with your decision making, as I believe that there are advantages and disadvantages to both.

Below are some questions I ask clients who are interested in switching from a typical mortgage loan to a HELOC. It is important to answer these questions honestly. If you had an extra $400 each month because you now have interest-only payments, would you do any of the following?

- Move into a bigger home?
- Dine out more often?
- Take more vacations?
- Buy a newer vehicle?
- Spend it on your kids?
- Buy more stuff?

If you answered yes to any of these questions, I would suggest that you stay away from home equity lines of credit. If you answered no to the above questions, and it makes sense financially, go for it.

5. Credit Consolidation Trap

Consolidating debt is when you take all of your debt and try and put it together under one account. Not only does this typically put your balances at more than 50 percent of the limit, but it can also hurt you in other ways.

Consolidating all the balances and freeing up some cash flow, or limits on other cards, can make it all too tempting to get into more debt. Please be aware that there is a very real danger of any one of us falling into the credit consolidation trap. We may start off with good intentions, but when it comes to finances, we seem to have short-term memories.

One way people consolidate debt is with balance transfers. These are low introductory rate offers that are only good for a limited time (e.g., six months to one year). Before you get too excited when you see the advertising of 1.9 to 3.9 percent being offered, be aware that there is some fine print. If you don't pay off your card in full at the expiry of the offer, your rates will jump from single digits to double digits, which are generally higher than your original interest rate. Remember, the banks are in the business of making money, and they are offering a "special rate" to you because they are hoping that you will be like the majority of their clients, who either don't pay off their balance, or they go into more debt because the interest rate is so low.

The goal of credit consolidation is to get your debt changed over to accounts that have low interest rates. The most common medium for consolidation seems to be with mortgage financing. The rates are lower due to the fact that the credit account is secured with a house, and so people mix their personal consumer debt with a mortgage or a HELOC. There is nothing wrong with doing this, and if you look at the numbers, it generally makes financial sense. The problem with consolidating your debts using your mortgage or other investments is that it is too easy. The habits that put you in that situation in the first place, most likely, haven't changed. Therefore, once you have successfully grouped the debt together, and lowered your payments, what are you tempted to do? Go shopping!

Unfortunately, there seems to be more "shopaholic" in us than most of us want to admit. If you have read the *Shopaholic* series of books written by Sophie Kinsella, or watched the movie, *Confessions of a Shopaholic*, you may be able to identify with the main character. This series follows Rebecca Bloomwood, a woman in her early 30s, who can't help but shop; it becomes her retail form of therapy. There is nothing wrong with credit consolidation, but there is a real danger if it is used to temporally relieve a guilty conscience, or make room for new purchases on your credit. Unlike the movie and books, debt or the unintentional desire to abuse credit, doesn't just disappear because you've found your soul mate, no matter how dreamy or rich he or she is.

Average Joe Action Steps

1. Honestly review how you've handled certain types of credit or money, and find out which type of credit works best for you.

2. If you are thinking of consolidating your debt, ask yourself first, "Have I changed the action that got me into debt in the first place?" If not, change what is causing the problem first and then look at consolidation as an option.

Six
Rule 5:
What You Don't Use,
You Lose!

You may think that once you've established your credit and you have a high score that you're good to go. The problem is that the credit reporting agencies who decide how each rule is weighed aren't the average Joe. This is how Equifax and TransUnion see it: No matter what type of credit account you use to establish your history, they want it kept active. If you stop using your accounts, they will eventually be deemed inactive. Inactive accounts don't hurt your credit; they just stop improving your score. Think of your credit like trying to walk up the down side of the escalator: At any point during the journey if you stop moving forward, you are eventually going to end up at the bottom again.

For those of you who are just starting to establish credit or rebuilding your credit, loans have one advantage I didn't mention in the previous chapter. They force you to pay, at least once each month. During the length of your loan, it is those payments that help keep that account established and active. The downside is that the moment you make your last payment, on any type of loan, it is no longer considered active. This statement may take the average Joe by surprise; I know it did me. I thought that a loan showing "paid in full" would enhance my credit rating. However, it doesn't. Each credit account, no matter what type it is, the more current the account the more heavily weighed the information is used.

Samples 1 and 2 include arrows to show you where to look on your own credit reports to find out the last time that each of your accounts was used.

Sample 1
Equifax: When Was Your Account Last Used?

Car Loan Ltd.

Phone Number: (555) 555-5555	**High Credit/Credit Limit:** 0000006936
Account Number: XXX 285	**Payment Amount:** $144.00
Association in Account: Joint	**Balance:** $7,161.00
Type of Account: Installment	**Past Due:** $2,312.00
Date Opened: 2007-02	**Date of Last Activity:** 2009-10
Status: Closed by Consumer	**Date Reported:** 2010-10

Months Reviewed:	No payment 30 days late
Payment History:	No payment 60 days late
	No payment 90 days late

Here is an example I used earlier that illustrates the bank's position on loans. In Rule 3 (see Chapter 4), I told you the story of Alex and how the Canadian Mortgage and Housing Corporation (CMHC) required him to put another $24,000 toward his down payment before he could be approved for his mortgage financing. CMHC decided this was necessary because it said he had weak credit. In addition to Alex's one active credit card, he also had several other loans or installment accounts, but they weren't active. He had a car and an RSP loan that he had previously paid off, one only two months beforehand. Like the average Joe, Alex thought that it would show better to the banks if the loans were paid. Alex guessed wrong, and because of that he had to pay the price, double the amount of down payment he wanted to put down.

A downside to revolving credit accounts, such as a credit card, is that you have to keep track of how often it gets used. However, the

Sample 2
TransUnion: When Was Your Account Last Used?

Your Bank

Account Number: ****123   **Type:** Revolving Account   **Opened:** 08/17/2005

Condition: (Open)   **Pay:** Paid as Agreed   **Reported:** 02/04/2012

Balance: ....   **Status:** Open   **Responsibility:**
Individual Account

High Balance: $10,000   **Payment:** $0 Monthly (due every month)

Terms: **Limit:**   **Past Due:**

Remarks: Line of Credit
Amt in High Credit Column (Disp 122 – 130 of Trade Segment) is Credit
Limit

Two-Year Payment History:
TransUnion
OK OK OK OK OK OK OK OK OK OK OK OK
Feb Mar Apr May Jun Jul Aug Sep Oct Nov Dec 11
OK OK OK OK OK OK OK OK OK OK OK OK
Feb Mar Apr May Jun Jul Aug Sep Oct Nov Dec 12

Six-Year Payment History:
30 Days Late: 0   60 Days Late: 0   90 Days Late: 0

---

advantage is that the account doesn't ever have to be closed or paid off. It can remain at a zero balance for a while and still be deemed active. My suggestion would be to use your revolving credit at least once every four to six months in order to keep it active.

If you have a hard time controlling revolving credit, I would suggest that you develop a plan to keep yourself from being able to access it too easily. For example, you can literally freeze your credit cards by storing your credit cards in a block of ice in your freezer. If you do try this, make sure you put a reminder on the calendar to thaw and use them occasionally. The balance doesn't have to be there long, but once used it will show up again on your credit report. This will keep that account active, and then you can continue using cash or a different credit account for most of your expenses. If you have a parent or partner who you trust, you could also ask him or her to hold onto the credit card or hide it from you until a specific date. That way you can protect yourself from the temptation of easy access and still keep your credit active.

While I was teaching a credit seminar at a university, I met a professor who shared his credit experience with me. After finishing his schooling and establishing his credit, this professor received a job offer in the United States, which he accepted. He lived in the US for a couple of years. When he returned to Canada, he couldn't get approved for a mortgage at his bank, even though he had a good, secure job lined up. While in the US, he hadn't kept his Canadian credit active, so his credit rating showed up as an R instead of a number. An R credit score is a reject beacon, which basically tells potential lenders that there is not sufficient active information or history to provide a score.

Don't confuse this R credit score with an (R) for a revolving credit account. It is often better to have some late payments show up on your history than not have any active payments. Underwriters (i.e., the people who decide whether or not your financing will be approved) understand that things happen in life and that there may be good reasons why payments were tardy. Therefore, they will often look past these things. However, with no repayment history to examine, it makes it very difficult for someone to be approved for any type of financing. There is no information to determine whether you are the type of person who makes your payments on time, or someone who doesn't make them at all!

The professor had to rent a house for six months before he found a bank that would overlook his newly re-established credit history. Most lending institutions will allow you to use international credit reports as established credit for mortgage financing. However, not all banks accept other forms of credit records in lieu of their own country's credit report. Also, not every country has a credit-reporting agency. Even if they do, you would need to obtain a copy of your report in a format that an underwriter in your own country can understand.

You don't have to leave the country for your credit to go inactive. Recently, I was working with a couple who was having problems getting approved. It didn't take long to see what the issue was. Crystal's credit score was more than 700 because she had been using her credit cards on a regular basis. Adam's score had taken a beating because he had stopped using his credit cards ever since he had taken a job working in the oil rigs about a year earlier. As he was providing all the family income, even though Crystal had great credit, she didn't earn any income to help qualify.

When Adam was in the oil rig camp he didn't have much need for credit and whenever he did need to make a purchase he used his Debit Visa which, as you learned in the last chapter, doesn't affect a person's credit at all. Luckily, once he learned this rule, he was able to improve his credit by using his credit cards once every couple of months instead of only using his Debit Visa.

No matter what type of financing you're looking for, nothing, and I mean nothing, is better than having a well-established credit score and an active credit history.

Average Joe Action Steps

1. If building or rebuilding, use your credit at least once a month. If you're only maintaining your credit, use it every four to six months, at a minimum.

2. Review your credit. If you have loans for the purpose of only building credit, look at opening revolving accounts to protect yourself from having to restart your credit over with each loan.

3. If you are planning on leaving the country for more than six months, make sure you keep your credit active while you are away.

Seven

Rule 6:
Be Careful with
Joint Credit

I was taught to always include my spouse in all our financial decisions. However, I've now learned that "joint credit" is something to stay away from until after your credit has been established. As you and your partner decide what works best for you, here is something to keep in mind. Each person must build his or her own credit and keep it active as long as he or she lives.

It is common for both men and women to take paternity and maternity leaves from work. So, what happens if your mortgage is up for renewal or you are applying for financing, and someone is on paternity or maternity leave or one of you is out of work? How are you going to qualify for financing if one of you doesn't have established credit? If you both have strong established credit, you will have many more options to keep you in the best financial position possible.

Here is a personal example on why both partners in a relationship should have established credit. My wife Jess stays at home and works very hard teaching and trying to keep our two very energetic toddlers from wreaking havoc on our house. She doesn't have a job outside of the home, but Jess helps my business with bookkeeping and other paperwork. She also has a couple of smaller, home-based businesses that she works on part time. Not only does she contribute to the family by raising our kids, but she also adds to the family income.

When our third bouncing bundle of joy was in the oven and our small car was not equipped to hold another car seat, we decided we needed to upgrade into what my wife refers to as a "Swagger Wagon." I guess that's a cooler way of saying minivan. Having followed the Nine Rules of Credit since our marriage began, she was automatically approved for a vehicle loan when she went in to meet with someone at the bank. She was in and out of the bank within 20 minutes, which is record timing with two toddlers in tow.

By getting the new vehicle on her own, Jess's action will be a huge help to me in the future when I may require more business or personal financing, as I won't have to include this purchase on my application. This in turn will allow me to be approved for a larger loan amount. It is also beneficial to have two incomes listed on an application, in order to help you qualify for higher loans, or possibly lower interest rates.

Some types of financing, such as mortgage financing, won't even allow you to use someone else's income on an application, unless that person has established credit. This means that once again, you may not qualify for the full amount of money that you need, or you may be charged a higher interest rate, because one of you didn't have your credit established.

1. The Pros of Joint Credit

Please don't misinterpret my warnings about the dangers of joint credit as meaning that holding credit together is always a bad thing. Joint credit can be a great tool. For example, it is common for one partner to utilize his or her credit more than another.

Joint credit can help keep each partner's credit active, which would have really helped Adam and Crystal's situation (see Chapter 6). If you remember that previous example from Rule 5, Adam didn't use his credit at all. If they had joint credit, his wife, who managed the family finances, could have kept it active for him. This would have prevented Adam's credit from going inactive.

2. The Cons of Joint Credit

Here's another example from one of my clients. Two years previously from meeting Jordan and Melanie they purchased two cars with the hopes to use the car loans to improve both their credit. Although, both names were added onto the loan, the company decided to report both car loans under Melanie's name. They had never reviewed their credit during those two years and just assumed that it was reporting under both of their names. Unfortunately, these car loans only built Melanie's credit and two years later Jordan still had no current credit reporting under his name on either TransUnion or Equifax. It didn't matter who was paying the loan or which account the money was coming from, it only matters what is showing up on the credit report.

I also had a personal experience that illustrates how the dangers of credit aren't isolated to just a husband and wife relationship. Before I went to South America, I had my father added to my credit card as a co-applicant. What I didn't know was that although the credit company issued my dad his own card, it was still my account, as I was the primary applicant. I would have been held responsible for everything my dad bought with his card, and had he not made his payments, it would have only affected my credit, not his. Initially, I thought adding my father to my credit account was a great way to keep my credit active while I was out of the country, but there was also a huge risk involved. What if my dad had decided to run off to Mexico? Making even the minimum payments would have been the last thing on his mind. Although my dad had a separate card, with a different credit card number, and only his name on it, I would have been held entirely responsible for any debt acquired.

Both of the above experiences are examples of when joint credit can be dangerous to your credit. In Jordan's case, although he was making the payments on the car loan, because the car company decided to put everything in Melanie's name, he wasn't building his credit. In my situation, because I had added another person onto the original account, and we didn't apply at the same time, good or bad it would affect only my credit and not my dad's. In addition, my dad would not be building his credit even if he was the one making the payments on time.

Another reason to be cautious with joint credit is just in case the nature of your relationship changes. For example, when a marriage ends in divorce or separation, it doesn't matter who spent the money. If the debt is registered on both of your credit reports, you are, individually, held 100 percent responsible for paying it off and making sure the minimum payment is paid.

Jessie, a credit repair client of mine, learned this the hard way. When she was younger, her boyfriend at the time was sold on the idea of purchasing an expensive vacuum. The problem was his credit was not very good so he could not qualify for the financing the company was offering. Jessie thought there would be no harm in adding her name to the contract. As time went on their relationship ended and they went their separate ways, but the vacuum stayed with him. Four years late Melanie had met a new man and was now engaged and was preparing to start their new lives together. They were looking into getting some vehicle financing together only to be declined due to a collection for $10,000 showing up on her credit report. It turns out that the ex-boyfriend had stopped making the payments a very long time ago and with all the fees and interest he had no interest in paying them back. It didn't matter that she didn't have the purchased item anymore or that he was supposed to be making the payments, the financing company came after both of them because both of their names were on the original contract.

It is also very common, when a couple separates or divorces, that one or both parties discontinue making payments on debt. Some stop making the minimum payment because they feel it isn't their responsibility anymore and others because their lawyers have told them to forego further payments. The downside to this is that even if you are officially divorced, you can't cancel or take your name off the account until either it is paid down to zero, or unless ordered to do so by the courts. You can try and freeze the account, but that doesn't always work. You can freeze your account by calling in a lost/stolen card or by asking the bank to verify if it will put a hold on the account. Even if a judge eventually rules in your favour about whose debt it really is, in the meantime, your personal credit will be a mess.

Death, divorce, and babies aren't the only things that can turn your financial life upside down. Life is always full of surprises, and you'll be thankful you were prepared for these times by following my advice. In short, I strongly advise everyone to have at least two personal credit accounts, because you never know what could happen to your partner. In addition to your personal credit, you can apply for some joint credit accounts, if you think it would help keep each other's accounts more active.

3. Find out How the Account Is Registered

Credit agencies and banks have never looked negatively on people's credit just because they have joint accounts, but you have to understand how to use joint credit properly. In order to do this, you need to know how each account is registered. The absolute only way of knowing how an account is reporting is by verifying it yourself. As knowledgeable as family, friends, and even some sales reps are, you need to see it for yourself.

Samples 3 and 4 include arrows to show you how you can tell if an account is joint with someone else or individually owned.

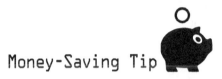

Money-Saving Tip

If you have one partner with good credit and the other with bad credit, try applying under only the name of the partner who has good credit. This will get you a lower interest rate, and thus save you money. However, this won't work if the person with bad credit earns all the money, and the person who has good credit doesn't. If you are applying for mortgage financing, talk to your mortgage professional to see what your options are.

Average Joe Action Steps

1. Review your credit reports to make sure you know how each credit account is reporting — joint or single.

2. If you don't have at least two credit accounts just in your name, make it happen.

Sample 3
Equifax: Joint Account

Car Loan Ltd.

Phone Number: (555) 555-5555

Account Number: XXX 285

Association in Account: Joint

Type of Account: Installment

Date Opened: 2007-02

Status: Closed by Consumer

High Credit/Credit Limit: 0000006936

Payment Amount: $144.00

Balance: $7,161.00

Past Due: $2,312.00

Date of Last Activity: 2009-10

Date Reported: 2010-10

Months Reviewed:

Payment History:

No payment 30 days late

No payment 60 days late

No payment 90 days late

Sample 4
TransUnion: Individual Account

Your Bank

Account Number: ****123	**Type:** Revolving Account	**Opened:** 08/17/2005
Condition: (Open)	**Pay:** Paid as Agreed	**Reported:** 02/04/2012
Balance:	**Status:** Open	**Responsibility:** Individual Account
High Balance: $10,000	**Payment:** $0 Monthly (due every month)	
Terms:	**Limit:**	**Past Due:**

Remarks: Line of Credit

Amt in High Credit Column (Disp 122 – 130 of Trade Segment) is Credit Limit

Two-Year Payment History:

TransUnion

OK OK OK OK OK OK OK OK OK OK OK OK

Feb Mar Apr May Jun Jul Aug Sep Oct Nov Dec 11

OK OK OK OK OK OK OK OK OK OK OK OK

Feb Mar Apr May Jun Jul Aug Sep Oct Nov Dec 12

Six-Year Payment History:

30 Days Late: 0	60 Days Late: 0	90 Days Late: 0

Eight

Rule 7:
Applying for Credit
Lowers Your Score

I am glad to see many of my clients are now asking about Rule 7 before they give their consent for a credit check. On your credit report, you will see the names of any one person or company who has checked your credit report. Some of these inquiries lower your score and some don't. Hard inquiries are made by commercial institutions, and not only do they lower your score, but other lenders will be able to see the names of these creditors. Soft inquiries don't lower your score and can't be seen by other creditors. Generally, soft inquiries are made by companies looking to make sure you are paying your bills on time but they aren't providing additional financing.

The exact number by which your score lowers due to a hard inquiry will depend on numerous factors, but generally it will be somewhere between five and ten points. Many people don't understand why just checking their score will lower it. The credit-reporting agencies, both Equifax and TransUnion, view the loss of five to ten points as something that won't make or break your credit, so they are not too concerned.

However, credit-reporting agencies make it very clear that they want to discourage people from applying for new credit regularly. That is why there is a practice of detracting points for a certain pattern of credit checks.

Equifax confirms this fact on its website by saying, "Even if you're just comparison-shopping for the best rate, too many inquiries can be viewed as a desperate bid to obtain credit to get out of financial trouble."

TransUnion explains it this way: "Each hard inquiry may cause a drop in your credit score. Multiple inquiries within a short amount of time, such as when you are shopping for a mortgage, are grouped together to lessen the impact. The actual impact depends on the number of inquiries, time period, and other factors on your credit profile."

Due to the reporting agencies' vague explanations, everyone seems to have a different opinion on the matter. Some of the confusion on the matter is due to the criteria being measured differently depending on the version of your credit report and if it is an Equifax and TransUnion report. With Equifax, when applying for mortgage or vehicle financing, any applications (inquiries) over the next 14 days will only lower your score as if you had pulled it once. With TransUnion, similar inquiries only lessen the impact rather than completely take away the consequence of lowering your credit score.

Multiple credit checks can also hurt your chances of being approved in ways other than by lowering your credit score. Some banks, especially for mortgages, may see recent inquiries as an indicator that you have new debt out there that has not yet been reported. For example, if you have had multiple credit checks from banks and vehicle companies, and now you are applying for a mortgage, the new lender may question if you have bought a vehicle that won't show up on your credit report for another 30 days.

The more you owe, the higher the risk you are to the banks. If lenders deem you too risky, they may charge you fees, higher interest rates, or even worse, turn you down. If a lot of inquiries for the same type of financing show up on your report, lending institutions may think you can't be approved elsewhere. If multiple companies have denied you, then why should another one accept you? Obviously, they will look at other key components, but it may cause the underwriter to take a closer look at your file.

I, like most people, don't see rate shopping as a bad thing because most of the time we're just trying to get the best possible financing package. It doesn't matter what type of financing you are applying for, whether it's the lowest rate for a credit card, a vehicle loan, or mortgage financing, a hard credit inquiry will affect your credit the same way.

In order to eliminate the risk of your score dropping with this rule; you can always pull your own credit report, make copies, and give one to everyone who needs one. This lets you and the sales rep know exactly what you look like on paper, and it doesn't affect your score. You can personally request your credit report as many times as you want to, and it won't register your name on the list of inquiries or have any other negative affect.

Here are a couple of examples on how making copies of your personal credit report can help in real-life situations. Let's say you're looking to buy a new vehicle and you want the best financing possible. Having your credit report in front of the lender will allow it to make a preliminary assessment on what amount it can offer you. However, if you should decide to go ahead with the financing, the lender will have to access your credit report and not just the copy. Although you will still have to get your credit checked, you can do all the shopping around you want before it lowers your score.

You can also use this system with mortgage financing. If you only know your score, a mortgage specialist can only give you a rough estimate of the best rate the banks may offer you, but a copy of your credit report, along with the score, will allow any mortgage professional to better know what you will qualify for. He or she should also be able to analyze the strengths and weaknesses of your credit report and advise you of any concerns a bank may have and how to resolve them.

The one type of financing I have not seen this method of pre-pulling your report work for is with credit cards. Most major banks, and even the small department stores, will ask you to call a toll-free number to apply. You can ask for a quote of its interest rates before you apply, but the general rule is that the company won't talk to you until it looks at your credit.

No matter what type of financing you are applying for, knowing the strength of your credit will give you peace of mind. It can also help you negotiate the best terms and conditions for your next financing package with confidence.

Money-Saving Tip

```
Call your credit card company to ask if it can lower
your rate. Most people have a hard time believing that
credit card rates are negotiable. A number of years
ago, I attended a real estate investment seminar with
about 90 people. One day, our homework was to call our
credit card companies and ask if we could get our rates
lowered. I made the call and was surprised when they
lowered mine from 19 percent to 12 percent. I thought I
had done an awesome job! The next morning, I found out
that about half of the class, who had also called their
credit card companies, had similar positive results. I
was really surprised to hear that some reported being
able to get their rates down as low as 6.5 percent, and
not just temporarily, as with a balance transfer.
```

Since that seminar, I have called my credit card companies and discovered that if you mention that you have received an offer from a competing credit card company, it will help you negotiate an even better interest rate with your existing credit card provider. If you want a benchmark rate to work from, you can always visit www.TheAverageJoeBook.com to find out competing rates and promotions from all the major credit card companies. Usually, credit card companies will advertise low rates to get more new customers, so you can use this to help you negotiate a lower interest rate. The worst the company can do is say no, and then you either continue with the same rate, or you try a different bank to see who will give you the best rate and terms.

1. Read the Fine Print before You Sign the Contract

Any time that you are asked to sign a contract, make sure you read the entire document carefully, especially the fine print. Even if you don't think a credit check is required for what you're applying for, it's always good to verify it. Whether it's for Air Miles, renting property, or to have an alarm system installed, you will need a credit check before you can be approved.

In the mortgage world, mortgage professionals are audited or reviewed by credit-reporting agencies every once in a while to ensure that they were given your written permission before checking your credit. Be cautious, though, as some companies don't ask for any type of confirmation from you before looking at your credit. Also, be aware that when you are dealing with companies that you have already worked with, most client contracts include a clause that allows lenders to check your credit without additional written consent. The only way you can guarantee that a company won't look at your credit without your consent is by not giving it your personal information to begin with.

The good news is that inquiries will eventually be removed from your credit report. However, both TransUnion and Equifax state a different time frame for this to happen. TransUnion says that "each hard inquiry will be displayed on your credit profile for a minimum of six years, but may remain longer." Equifax doesn't put as much emphasis on a full six years for inquiries. It says, "The following inquiries were generated because the listed company has requested a copy of your credit report. An inquiry, made by a Creditor, will automatically purge three years from the date it is made. The system will keep record of a minimum of 5 inquiries." This means that you may see inquiries prior to the three-year date on your report, but that is only if you don't have five recent inquiries made within the last three years.

The average Joe isn't the only one who doesn't know how an inquiry can affect credit. Unfortunately, neither do the majority of sales reps calling you from companies, large or small. That means it is completely up to you to protect your personal information. Only you can prevent the lowering of your score by having too many credit checks done.

Average Joe Action Steps

1. Next time you apply for credit, print a copy of your credit report and use it to shop for the best interest rates.

2. Read the fine print on any application because you could be giving someone permission to check your credit now and in the future.

Nine
Rule 8:
Closing Your Credit
Accounts Lowers
Your Score

Ever cut up your credit cards or close your credit accounts? Closing any type of credit account can reduce your score dramatically. This is an area where people who think they know the rules of credit get hurt the most often. I find that the average Joe understands that he or she must pay his or her bills on time, but the person doesn't realize that cancelling credit accounts will affect his or her credit negatively.

It won't matter what the reason is because the predetermined computer code, which the credit-reporting agencies use, shows a cancelled credit account as a negative. Many argue that this rule doesn't make any sense. Unfortunately, credit-reporting agencies don't take into consideration that you're trying to protect yourself by cancelling your credit.

When I first started in the mortgage industry, I found out the hard way exactly how important Rule 8 is and how much it can lower your score. I met Rob and Elise when they were looking to purchase a new property. When he and his wife sat down with me, and we went over the numbers, everything looked good, so I requested their credit reports, and both their scores were fine. We submitted the application to the bank for the purchase and everything was approved and ready to go.

A problem arose, however, as they applied for a home equity line of credit for their existing home, through their bank. They acquired this financing in order to have a larger down payment for their new property. Everything went smoothly except when it came closer to the final weeks before they were to move. About five months after I had originally reviewed their credit, the bank with which I had the mortgage approved on the new house, asked me to get an updated credit report. When I looked at Rob's new credit score, it had dropped 50 points lower than the first time I checked.

I wondered what he had done wrong, so I compared his first credit report to the new one. Everything seemed to be exactly the same. No missed payments, no increase of funds, and no new credit. The only difference was that a credit card and a personal line of credit had been closed. What I didn't know was that part of the condition for them to get the home equity line of credit with his current bank required him to close two credit accounts he had with competing banks. Rob had no clue this would hurt his credit. Although he'd had those credit accounts for a while, he didn't use them much anymore because he had newer credit cards that offered him rewards and a lower interest rate. However, Rob and Elise's ability to qualify for the type of mortgage product and rate they were looking for on the purchase had been based on them being in a certain category with their credit scores. Now, because of this huge drop in Rob's score, they no longer qualified. After a lot of explaining, producing of documentation, and even a little bit of begging, an exception was made. The saving grace was that these accounts, which their bank made them cancel, weren't joint accounts. They were only in Rob's name, leaving Elise's score the same.

It is quite common for banks and mortgage companies to request that you pay off debt so that you can qualify, but asking you to close accounts with competitor's is another thing all together. If you notice that this is one of the conditions of your mortgage, talk to your mortgage rep about working around it. If the bank tells you that there is no way around it, you can always apply at another bank. At the very least, you will be aware that if you close credit accounts, your score is going to drop and it will take some time for it to come back up.

As bad as closing your credit accounts are for your credit score, it is even worse if the financial institution has to do it for you! This only happens when there is a problem with your account, which is generally caused by several late payments. The most common reasons people find themselves in this situation is because they either thought they had already paid off the balance, or they felt they weren't responsible for the outstanding amount in the first place. No matter what the situation is, closing or cancelling credit cards or lines of credit will affect your credit negatively. Remember that a bad credit history will not be erased just because you closed the offending account. This can still be viewed for many years after you have closed it.

1. Be Aware of "Upgrading" or Changing Your Credit Accounts

Even if you are "upgrading" your card, you may be hurting your credit. I made this mistake with my longest-running credit card. Before I knew the Nine Rules of Credit, I upgraded my basic Visa credit card to a "Gold" status, which offered rewards. What I didn't know was that the bank had my old card listed as "closed by consumer" on my credit report, and that the Gold Visa was now a brand new account.

Banks don't do this to purposefully hurt our credit; they do it to keep their systems organized. However, credit card and bank employees will swear to you that it won't hurt your credit. Now that you know this rule you can educate them!

Although my wife and I had a great vacation paid partially with my reward points, my repayment history with my longest-running credit card was now gone. That is more than 85 months (seven years and one month) of credit history wasted in one phone call. Knowing what I know now, I would have told the bank that I wanted to keep the old card and to sign me up for a new one too. That way I could have used the old card once every six months just to keep it active, and the new card for the majority of my spending.

This warning applies to loans as well, which happens most commonly with vehicle financing. If you switch financing from one vehicle to another or even increase the loan amount on your existing account, the bank will close that account and start a new one. This has the same affect that closing any type of account does.

Another growing trend happening today is that people are closing their credit accounts in fear of identity theft. It is true that inactive credit accounts are targets for fraudsters. However, this can be controlled by actively checking your balances, instead of closing your accounts. You can stop using your account or cut up your credit card, and after one or two years, your account will be deactivated.

If you have to close an account, I advise you not to do so if you're going to apply for credit in the near future. This will give your score time to rebound, before you apply for any new credit. As stated in Rule 3, when closing any credit account, make sure you still have at least two established accounts. By signing up for a new card with a point or reward system, you may get that dream trip faster, but you may also be losing your credit status at the same time.

It also matters which credit account you choose to cancel or go inactive. The longer you have had the credit account established, the more it will hurt your credit when you cancel it. When reviewing your credit, you can see the status or condition of each account.

Although the age of the applicant is irrelevant to your credit report, it makes sense that the longer you can prove a clean active payment history, the less risky you become to the banks. Ending or upgrading any credit account will effectively stop the clock on how long your credit has been established.

Samples 5 and 6 include arrows to show you the status of your account.

Average Joe Action Step

1. Review your credit reports to see which accounts have been established the longest and avoid cancelling or upgrading them.

Sample 5
Equifax: Status of Account

Car Loan Ltd.

Phone Number: (555) 555-5555   **High Credit/Credit Limit:** 0000006936

Account Number: XXX 285   **Payment Amount:** $144.00

Association in Account: Joint   **Balance:** $7,161.00

Type of Account: Installment   **Past Due:** $2,312.00

Date Opened: 2007-02   **Date of Last Activity:** 2009-10

Status: Closed by Consumer   **Date Reported:** 2010-10

Months Reviewed: No payment 30 days late

Payment History: No payment 60 days late

                            No payment 90 days late

Sample 6
TransUnion: Status of Account

Your Bank

Account Number: ****123   **Type:** Revolving Account   **Opened:** 08/17/2005

Condition: (Open)   **Pay:** Paid as Agreed   **Reported:** 02/04/2012

Balance: ....   **Status:** Open   **Responsibility:**
                                                              Individual Account

High Balance: $10,000   **Payment:** $0 Monthly (due every month)

Terms: **Limit:**   **Past Due:**

Remarks: Line of Credit
Amt in High Credit Column (Disp 122 – 130 of Trade Segment) is Credit Limit

Two-Year Payment History:

TransUnion

OK OK OK OK OK OK OK OK OK OK OK OK

Feb Mar Apr May Jun Jul Aug Sep Oct Nov Dec 11

OK OK OK OK OK OK OK OK OK OK OK OK

Feb Mar Apr May Jun Jul Aug Sep Oct Nov Dec 12

Six-Year Payment History:

30 Days Late: 0   60 Days Late: 0   90 Days Late: 0

Ten
Rule 9:
Protect Yourself

As I've mentioned before, it can take years to build your credit, but it doesn't take long to destroy it. Sometimes it isn't even a lack of knowledge or poor money management that can ruin your credit score, forcing you to start over. It is becoming more common for someone else to hurt your credit for you. That is why the last, and very important rule, is to protect your credit.

1. Protect Your Personal Information

Don't throw away your statements. Buy a good paper shredder so that no one can use your personal information. This advice is not just for businesses, but also for the average Joe.

When I began in the mortgage industry, I knew that legally I had to dispose of sensitive information by shredding it. It wasn't until after learning about credit that I started to use the shredder for my own personal documents too.

To better understand the importance of this, take a look at some of your financial statements, and then try to imagine what a criminal could do with them. Your name, address, phone numbers, and even part of your account numbers could be used by a fraudster to take advantage of you. If your wallet is stolen, you usually notice right away, and you can have your accounts cancelled quickly. Most financial statements come out once a month or on a quarterly basis. Just imagine how much harm a criminal could do over a period of one month.

There are many ways and programs to protect yourself online, but the best method is to review your financial statements regularly. This is something I'm a little lazy about myself, but fortunately for me, my wife is much more diligent. Regular reviews will not only protect you against fraud, but from human or computer error as well. I often see mistakes on people's credit reports, and generally, by the time I let them know about them, extensive delays have prevented them from being approved for financing quickly.

Your personal information needs to be protected not only in paper form, but in all aspects. Be careful what information you confirm over the phone. If someone calls you and asks you for your personal information, don't give it to him or her, even if it's a reputable company. If the person is calling to verify your information with simple yes and no questions, then it's probably not a big deal. What you should do if you're in doubt is hang up and dial the number on the back of your bank card or credit card to verify the information. This way you know for sure who you're talking to. If you have to speak to a specific agent, get his or her full name before you hang up. Then, when you call back, you can ask for that person directly.

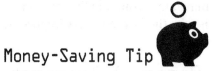

Money-Saving Tip

The Better Business Bureau has estimated that identity theft may cost consumers, banks, credit card firms, stores, and other businesses more than $2 billion annually. No matter whether you have fraud insurance or protection on your credit accounts or not, it is still a cost that eventually gets passed along to us, the average Joe consumer. Do you want to save money? Then protect your credit and information, as this is one of the fastest growing crimes in North America.

2. Social Insurance Number (SIN)

Your Social Insurance Number (SIN) is very important, as it easily identifies you. It is the only piece of identification that won't be the same as anyone else's. It is a no-brainer that you should keep your number from being lost or stolen.

Although it's important to keep your number safe, remember that on almost all credit applications nothing can be submitted or finalized without your SIN. That is why it is so important to find out who you are working with before you give out any information.

It always surprises me how liberal people are with their personal information. For anyone who has applied for a mortgage, you will know how much personal information the banks require for financing. When I had a mortgage website, people would divulge their personal information before even checking on me because they wanted the rate that was being offered. I have had more than a few clients, after gathering all the information necessary to process a mortgage application, joke that I now knew more about them than they did!

3. Basic Ways to Protect Yourself

Although the police and governing bodies are constantly trying to catch fraudsters, here are some basic ways to protect yourself:

- Find out who you are dealing with before you send any information.

- Take the sales rep information and the business information and verify it.

- You can contact the Better Business Bureau (BBB) to see if the information you have received matches with its information.

- Type into a search engine "fraudulent companies in Canada" and you will find numerous websites designed to report and warn about popular scams.

- Check government and association websites to verify their information:

  - Canadian Anti-Fraud Centre: www.antifraudcentre.ca

  - Royal Canadian Mounted Police (RCMP) — Scams and Fraud: www.rcmp-grc.gc.ca/scams-fraudes/index-eng.htm

If you are dealing with professionals within a certain industry, you can verify their information based on their governing body. Governing bodies are organizations, which exist solely to bring and maintain a certain level of standard of whatever professional category they are in. Some have websites that are designed specifically for the general public. For example, for mortgages, almost every jurisdiction has a governing body that each person in that field has to be registered. You can easily check on an agent's status or make a complaint on these websites. Generally, it's as easy as putting in the person's last name to view his or her status and contact information. By no means is this a complete list, but even by being a bit more aware, it will help you keep your credit safe.

Please note that all of the links to these websites can also be found on my website (www.TheAverageJoeBook.com). For the most up-to-date news on different scams you can also follow me on Facebook (https://www.facebook.com/theaveragejoebook).

4. Get Everything in Writing

Don't *ever* take someone's word for it; get it in writing. It is very common to have bills or collections continue reporting as unpaid even though they have been paid. The problem is that you can't prove that you have paid a debt if you don't have something in writing. When working with banks, it means nothing unless you have written proof.

The other key point to keep in mind is once you have received written confirmation, keep it somewhere safe. Having documentation will also reduce the amount of time it takes to have the credit-reporting agencies remove the error from your reports.

One of my clients, Dave, had a collection of approximately $8 on his credit report. Every six months or so, he would get a bill from a cell phone company for an account that had been closed years earlier. He just kept paying it, because he couldn't quite remember if he had paid the bill before, and he thought a bill of less than $10 wasn't worth fighting over. Each time he paid it, the clerk assured him that the account was now paid in full. Dave's problem was that he didn't get confirmation in writing. The bills stopped coming only once he demanded to receive written confirmation of his bill payment. If you are in a situation like Dave was, don't pay unless the charging company can give you something in writing, stating that the account has a zero balance. After a couple of months, you would be wise to verify that it has been taken off of your credit report. I guarantee you that no one else is going to follow up on your account to make sure everything is recorded properly. That is completely up to you.

5. Be Careful of Credit-Fixing Scams

Just like in every other industry there are credit-fixing companies that promise you the world but don't live up to what they are selling. Here are some ways to help protect yourself. Make sure that the credit-fixing company is based in Canada. It is a lot harder to verify a company's validity and credibility if it is located in a different country.

It is always best to work with a company that has a good reputation and one that was recommended to you by someone you know personally. If you don't know of anyone who has used that company's services before, you can always ask a professional in the finance industry for recommendations. Trustees, financial planners, and mortgage brokers are great sources to point you in the right direction. Check into the company and see if it is credible. You can also put the companies name in a search engine online with the letters "BBB" and you will pull up its Better Business Bureau profile which will show any complaints.

After I finished and self-published the first version of this book, I had many people asking for me to find a company that would help remove errors or fraud from their credit reports and also improve their credit. After looking for a solution for my clients I couldn't find a trusted name across Canada that just focused on removing errors or fraud from credit reports or improving a credit score quickly. That is why in 2012, I stopped focusing on mortgage financing and started developing a system that would help people with all aspects of their credit. Once the development of the system was complete I started the company called eCredit Fix. Although I am 100 percent biased, I now suggest eCredit Fix for any Canadians who need to easily and inexpensively improve their credit score to remove errors or fraud from their credit reports.

6. Secured Credit Better than Cosigning

I think that we're all somewhat aware of how dangerous it is for fraudsters to get a hold of our credit, but what about the possibility of our loved ones unwittingly wreaking havoc with it? If you're trying to help a spouse, a child, or some other relative establish credit, I would recommend that you get him or her started with a secured card instead of cosigning with him or her.

A secured credit card, unlike cosigning, can limit your risk because the only loss to you would be whatever amount you put as a deposit for another person. When cosigning, you are attaching your name to someone else's account, so if a payment isn't made, it will affect both person's credit. Cosigning won't automatically hurt your credit, but just like joint credit, you will be held 100 percent responsible for the activities on that account no matter who is at fault. As important as establishing credit is, keep in mind that for some people, especially the inexperienced, credit can be a recipe for disaster. The risks and extra costs of cosigning can be learned from the following experience.

Eric, who was self-employed, was applying for a mortgage. For those of you who are self-employed, the major banks want to see an even better credit score than from those who are employees. In this case, Eric was just under the minimum required credit score to qualify through a major bank. When I asked him about the one credit card that showed a very poor credit repayment history, he told me that it was a card he had cosigned for his nephew. Due to this card and the very tight qualifying restrictions he was under, he had to get his mortgage from a smaller lender who charged him a 1.35 percent higher interest rate and a 4 percent additional fee. This may not seem like a lot, but over five years, it cost him an extra $54,733.19 on his mortgage.

Sometimes, the banks will make exceptions when there is a good explanation, but in this case, because of other exceptions needing to be made on his file the major banks wouldn't approve him. I advised him that he should pay the balance on that joint card and close it. Although this would have fixed his credit and saved him money in the long term, he didn't want to do it. He didn't like the fact that he would be giving his nephew a way out of his responsibilities. I have to commend Eric for his resolve on the principle he was trying to instill in his nephew. However, in the meantime, his credit will continue to suffer until either his nephew learns to manage his credit or until the account is closed.

7. Fraud-Watch Programs

Both Equifax and TransUnion are very active in advertising their fraud-watch programs. Are they necessary? No! Can they be beneficial? You bet! I believe that for those of you who are rebuilding your credit or who are a bit lazy when it comes to reviewing your statements, these programs can help you.

Basically, each of these fraud-watch programs gives you access to your individual credit reports, notifies you of any irregular activity, and gives you 24/7 access to an agent to help you understand what is happening on your account. Each of these programs will cost you about $15 a month. If you are interested in finding out more on what is offered by each credit reporting agency please visit their websites for more details.

No matter if you sign up for one of these programs or not, it is very important to protect and review your credit constantly. I would suggest that you review your credit report at least once a year with each reporting agency. This will insure that you can correct errors quickly and always maintain amazing credit.

8. The Nine Rules of Credit

That's it; the Nine Rules of Credit that the average Joe needs to know in order to start, rebuild, and maintain excellent credit. Not to worry though, it isn't the end of this book. Please keep in mind that although I call these the Nine Rules of Credit, sometimes it's necessary to follow your rebellious instincts and break a few of them in order to achieve something bigger. For example, opening multiply credit accounts will lower your credit score. However, if you don't have credit, then opening a few accounts are necessary.

Don't get me wrong; every time you break a rule, it brings negative consequences. However, being aware of these rules puts you in control by letting you weigh the advantages as well as the risks before making your decision. You can also limit mistakes and speed up your recovery time now that you understand how the credit reporting agencies grade you. It's kind of like writing an open-book test and having a cheat sheet. Don't worry, though, this isn't being dishonest. It's just playing to win!

Average Joe Action Steps

1. Devise a plan to review your credit and accounts regularly.

2. Review the Nine Rules of Credit on a regular basis so you don't forget them.

Eleven
The Big Picture

The quote, "The only thing constant in life is change" applies to your credit score as well as life. Each month, any action or inaction will change your credit score. I've included this chapter to help recap the Nine Rules of Credit, but also to illustrate how one transaction can affect your credit both positively and negatively at the same time. You will see a basic visual example of how each of the Nine Rules of Credit is weighed to make up your final credit score in the tables included in this chapter.

The power that comes from not only knowing the rules, but how important each one is, will put you in the driver's seat and allow you to make the best decisions possible regarding your credit.

1. How a Loan Can Affect Your Credit

Using the credit categories pie graph illustrated in Table 2, I will demonstrate how the basic action of applying for a loan can affect your credit. I will also refer back to my earlier story about the "Swagger Wagon" my wife bought. To understand the effects of this new loan on my wife's credit, you will need to know how her credit looked both before and after she applied. Previous to applying, Jess requested a copy of both her credit reports so she could, confidently, shop around for the best interest rates without having her credit checked each time. The numbers and results below are based on the information taken from her Equifax report. Her TransUnion Report reflected a similar scenario, except the score was a bit higher due to small differences between the two agencies. The main categories were ranked alike by both reporting agencies, with just a few minor differences.

Please keep in mind that Table 3 is a generic display of the main categories and a basic review of the Nine Rules of Credit. Equifax and TransUnion are competitors, so they will not openly reveal the exact algorithm they each use. The algorithm or electronic code that each reporting agency uses is also constantly upgraded to better reflect credit risk for the lending institutions.

Table 3
Credit Categories

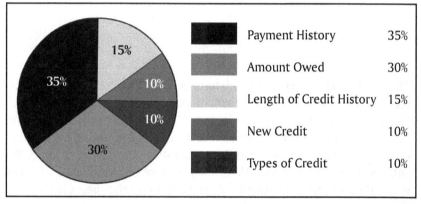

Payment History		35%
Amount Owed		30%
Length of Credit History		15%
New Credit		10%
Types of Credit		10%

1.1 Before the loan application

Before this loan application, Jess had three credit accounts, which included two different credit cards and a line of credit. The categories found in Tables 4 and 5 are the same ones found in the previously shown Table 3, only with further explanations written below them. I have also added a column named "Mark," so you can see how she was doing with each rule or category. This mark is based on a scale of one to ten, ten being the best.

Table 4
Credit Report Card:
Jess's Credit before the Loan

Credit Category	Credit Rule Number	Percent Weight	Mark
Payment history	1, 5, 9	35%	10
Amount owed	2, 9	30%	10
Length of credit history	3, 6, 8, 9	15%	9
New credit	7, 9	10%	10
Types of credit	4, 9	10%	7
Credit Score: 799			

Reasons for each mark are explained as follows:

- **Payment history:** Jess had never been late or missed a payment on any of her accounts. Although she used her accounts often, one of them hadn't been used during the past six months. Because two out of three accounts were active and she had a perfect payment history, she received a mark of ten out of ten. If she would have had a late payment within the last 12 months, it would have lowered her score by about 40 to 50 points. Multiple late payments, or even missed payments, would have really lowered her score. Missing her payments all together would have led to a collection company registering a collection on her credit report, which would have lowered her score by approximately 100 points.

- **Amount owed:** Her balances had never been more than 50 percent of her credit limits. This may be due to the fact that whenever she made large purchases, they always seemed to magically appear on my credit card rather than on hers! In this category, if the balance of one of her accounts had been closer to her limits, it would have dropped her score by 20 to 30 points. If her balance ever went over her limit, her score would have been reduced by at least 30 to 40 points.

- **Length of credit history:** The average time that her credit accounts had been open was 52 months (four years and four months); her newest account being established for just over three years. All limits were $2,500 or higher. Had each account been active for at least five years, this would have put her mark at ten out of ten, rather than nine out of ten. Although having a credit limit of $2,500 or more doesn't matter to your credit score, as you learned in Rule 3, a credit card limit of $500 doesn't look very established to banks and lenders.

- **New credit:** Jess had five inquiries made over the last seven years. When a lending institution looks at your credit, one hard inquiry (credit inquiries made by lenders that lower your score), or no inquiries each year, is considered really good.

- **Types of credit:** As previously mentioned, Jess had three accounts, all of them revolving, and one of them being a line of credit. She had no loans or open type accounts (e.g., cell phone account, Diners Club card). Since she only had revolving accounts (i.e., credit cards or lines of credit), it dropped her mark for this section to seven out of ten. Luckily for Jess, this account only weighs in up to a max of 10 percent of her credit score. This is why she still had such a high credit score.

Based on the Nine Rules of Credit, Jess was doing an awesome job of keeping her score high. The only three ways she could have improved her points would have been by using her one inactive account at least every four to six months, and by having all of her accounts established longer than five years. Having different types of credit, such as a loan, would have increased her mark in this category, but not very much overall. Having done really well with the majority of the rules, Jess's credit score was 799, which is considered "amazing." She makes me so proud!

1.2 After the loan application

Now, here is what happened once she applied and was approved for the new "Swagger Wagon" loan (see Table 5).

Table 5
Credit Report:
Jess's Credit after the Loan

Credit Category	Credit Rule Number	Percent Weight	Up	Down	N/A	New Mark	Old Mark
Payment history	1, 5, 9	35%			X	10	10
Amount owed	2, 9	30%		X		8	10
Length of credit history	3, 6, 8, 9	15%		X		7	9

New credit	7, 9	10%		X		9	10
Types of credit	4, 9	10%	X			10	7
Credit Score: 752							

Reasons for each mark are explained as follows:

- **Payment history:** No change would have occurred in this area as there weren't any missed payments and the new loan for the minivan is considered active.

- **Amount owed:** Remember, Equifax and TransUnion don't necessarily care how much someone owes; they are more concerned about the ratio of your balance compared to that of your limit. They feel that this is a better indicator of whether you are a credit risk or not. According to what we discussed in Rule 2, it is ideal to have your balance amounts at 50 percent or less on each of your account limits. Let's say that Jess was approved for a loan amount of $15,000. That means, as of day one, she would still owe $15,000. Remember, the price of the vehicle or the amount of your down payment is irrelevant when considering your credit. Therefore, her credit limit and balance will stay the same until she makes her first payment. Because her balance is 100 percent of what she borrowed on the original loan, her credit will be negatively affected until she has paid off at least half of it. Although loans can be borrowed for different lengths of time, in this example, the loan is for a period of five years. This means that the loan will lower her credit score for just over two-and-a-half years. It is in this category that her score will be hurt the most because it is weighed so heavily!

  How do you get around obtaining a vehicle loan and not having it hurt your credit? You can look at using a line of credit as long as your limit is high enough to accommodate the balance needed. The other option is to get approved for the highest loan amount possible by putting the lowest down payment up front. After you have the loan, apply as much money available to lower the balance. Since your credit score is a summary of all your accounts, if you need to apply for financing that may lower your score, the better established your other accounts are, the less it will reduce your score.

- **Length of credit history:** Jess's score would also be lowered in this category due to her opening a new account. As mentioned before, the credit-reporting agencies want to see your accounts established for as long as possible, but state that the ideal amount of time would be more than four years. I noted earlier that Jess had two of her accounts longer than four years. However, she also had a newer account for just over three years. This made the average time of her accounts being opened only four years and three months. Because she now had a new vehicle loan, it lowered the average time her credit had been established. Since length of credit is the third heaviest weighed category (i.e., 15 percent), new credit can also put a dent in the total score.

- **New credit:** New credit, although important, only makes up 10 percent of a person's total score, as explained more thoroughly in Rule 7. Jess's score would be lowered anywhere between five and ten points, by having one hard inquiry made (which is when a lending institution checks her credit). Based on the fact that she has had very few inquiries done in the past, I would estimate that this one inquiry only lowered her score by five points.

- **Types of credit:** The one positive increase to her score was found in this category. Unfortunately for Jess, this category only makes up a maximum of 10 percent of her credit score. However, this new loan will increase her credit score because both TransUnion and Equifax see obtaining and managing a selection of different types of credit as a sign of credit strength. As long as Jess maintains this new loan as well as she has her other accounts, it will show that she is responsible enough to manage this new installment, loan payment as well as her revolving trade lines, her credit cards, and line of credit.

My wife's score, even after dropping from 799 to 752, was OK because she received a great interest rate, got the van she wanted, and still is in the "amazing" credit category. However, this story wouldn't have been of the "happily ever after" variety if Jess's credit hadn't been so strong. It doesn't take much to reduce your score and put you in a category that could cost you more, or even keep you from being approved. Also, keep in mind that I reviewed her credit right after the new loan showed up, so with each month that she puts between her and the new credit account, her score will improve.

This is why I am so passionate about credit. There is nothing common about how the credit-reporting agencies rank your everyday actions in regards to being credit worthy. If knowing about credit and how it can affect you isn't common sense, and you obviously don't learn about it in school, then how does the average Joe learn about credit? The answer is this. You either go through life completely unaware or you learn the hard way, through personal experience.

I hope I have helped you understand that credit is a tool. Credit, like money, is designed to be used, but just as Sir Isaac Newton stated, "To every action there is always an equal and opposite reaction." There is nothing wrong with applying for a loan or any other type of credit, but there is a reaction for every action or inaction with credit. My goal is to protect you from making any unconscious mistakes.

Average Joe Action Step

1. If you want to understand how each action or inaction is affecting your score, you can compare past credit reports with your new ones to see what has changed.

Twelve
Some Important Things to Remember

Your credit score is only one determining factor when it comes to judging your eligibility for financing. Other contributing factors are known as the "Five Cs of Credit." The following are the five most important categories for the banks and lenders when they are checking to see if you qualify for additional credit:

1. **Character (Credit):** Your credit score and how established your credit is will help the banks determine your character. They want to see what the likelihood is of you paying them back. This book explains in great detail everything that would be considered to fall in this category. As banks, lenders, insurance companies, employers, landlords, and Canadians focus more on the credit score and report, this category is becoming more and more important to understand.

2. **Capacity:** The banks want to see that you are able to afford your current monthly payment responsibilities in addition to the new payment. They take how much you earn and compare it to how much you owe.

3. **Capital:** This is also known as a down payment or money down. It is money or assets that reduce the new lender's risk of you not making your payments. When times get tough, the more you personally stand to lose the less risk there is for the lender.

4. **Conditions:** This refers to the overall economic conditions of where you live and what the financing is being used for. You may have a great job and income working in a vehicle factory, but if there are plans to shut it down in the next year, it will affect your ability to qualify. You may currently have the "capacity" to make the payments right now; however, next year that would change, which would increase the risk for the bank.

5. **Collateral:** The collateral is the asset that the loan is attached to such as a vehicle, a house, or an investment. The value and condition the asset is in can either reduce the prospective lender's risk or increase it.

Each bank weighs each category differently depending on what type of financing you want to acquire. If you are weak in one category but you are stronger in the other categories, the better your chances of being approved. However, banks consider your credit (character) as one of the most important factors for qualifying.

1. Fixing Errors Found on Your Credit Reports

Almost everyone in Canada has errors or will have errors on their credit reports sometime during their lives. Fraud is part of the problem but a lot of times it is wrong or outdated information getting attached to your credit file. There are two ways for your to fix errors, you can do it yourself or you can have someone else do it for you. If you embark on doing it yourself, remember there is a learning curve and it can be a very frustrating process. From what I have heard from clients it is a very painful process and it takes about 20 hours, with multiple attempts, over about a six-month time frame to have it properly corrected. If that doesn't sound like fun to you, visit www.eCreditFix.ca to find easy and inexpensive solutions to quickly fix and improve your credit.

If Equifax or TransUnion have done an investigation, and there is still not enough evidence in your favour, you can always have a note added to your file. I would suggest adding a note only if the error was due to extenuating circumstances that you think future creditors should know about. These notes won't change your credit score but they will allow you to tell your side of the story. For example, you are aware that you were late on your credit card payment. However, this was because you just started a new job and the payroll department didn't have your correct banking information and, therefore, couldn't deposit your paycheque. Both credit-reporting agencies have guidelines that must be followed in order to post a comment on your credit report.

TransUnion states this on its website: "If our investigation does not resolve the dispute, you may add a 100-word consumer statement to your report. Exception: 200 words in Saskatchewan. Statements should be relevant to the credit information in dispute. Please note that TransUnion will not accept statements that are defamatory or otherwise illegal or inappropriate. Requests for statements to be added or removed should be placed in writing with your signature on them."

Equifax states this about credit disputes: "In either case, you may add a statement to our file explaining any concerns you have. Equifax will include your statement on all future credit reports, if it contains 400 words or less." Although Equifax doesn't include a warning in its notes, it will also disregard any comments that are graphic or contentious in nature. Try to keep all emotion out of your statement.

2. Your Debt Is Hurting Your Credit

When you are struggling with high debt loads it is very stressful and it can bring down many other aspects of your life as well. Some of my clients are unable to improve their credit due to their debt load so the first step is to use the available tools and government programs that can help them.

There are companies that can walk you through all the options that are available to assess the pros and cons of each one and walk you through the whole process. Be careful though, as many debt and counselling companies may advertise that they can help save your credit but some do more damage than good. If you have, or someone you know has, debt problems, you can find solutions, tools, and resources at www.TheAverageJoeBook.com under the "Debt" tab.

Average Joe Action Step

1. If you find that you have any missed payments, and it was due to circumstances beyond your control, add a note to your credit files with both TransUnion and Equifax.

Conclusion

Now that you have read this book, it is time for you to put the Nine Rules of Credit into practice. You may still have some questions about the subject, but I didn't write this book with the intent of making you all experts. My hope is to help you to understand the importance of credit, to learn the Nine Rules of Credit, and to motivate you to continue to monitor your credit. If you haven't requested copies of both your credit reports, now is the time to do so.

Like you, I have noticed that there is a great lack of knowledge and understanding when it comes to credit. How would anyone know about the rules required to be involved in the credit game? We don't learn these rules in school, and no one sat you down and gave you the "credit talk" when you were 18! I'd bet some parents would rather give their kids the "birds and bees" talk instead of the credit speech!

There are many books, websites, blogs, and TV segments that offer you tidbits of information from here or there, but everyone seems to be giving different advice. I hope you see the value of this book in understanding exactly how each of the Nine Rules of Credit affect your credit score and how best to quickly repair and maintain your score throughout your lifetime.

Here are some of the things that you will find on my website (www. TheAverageJoeBook.com):

- Direct links to free credit reports and other products for both Equifax and TransUnion.

- Videos on how to read your credit reports.

- Canadian Financial calculators to help you with mortgage and loan payments, comparing prepayment options , debt repayment, and more.

- Links to other good financing websites and blog posts that focus on credit and other financial education.

- Book list of other good books that deal with various financial subjects.

If you have any questions, feel free to email me at Richard@The AverageJoeBook.com.

Thank you for reading my book and good luck to you in all of your financial endeavours! From one average Joe to another, I genuinely care!